Gender at Work

Edited & Introduced by ANN MESSENGER

Gender at Work

FOUR WOMEN WRITERS OF THE EIGHTEENTH CENTURY

Wayne State University Press Detroit

Library of Congress Cataloging-in-Publication Data
Gender at work : four women writers of the eighteenth century / edited
   and introduced by Ann Messenger.
         p.   cm.
   Includes bibliographical references.
   ISBN 0-8143-2147-X (alk. paper)
   1. Women and literature—Great Britain—History—18th century.
   2. English literature—Women authors—History and criticism.
   3. English literature—18th century—History and criticism.
   4. Women authors, English—18th century—Biography. 5. Winchilsea,
Anne Kingsmill Finch, Countess of, 1661–1720. 6. Pilkington,
Laetitia, 1712–1750. 7. Pix, Mary, 1666–1720. 8. Darwall, Mary, 1738–1825.
   I. Messenger, Ann, 1933–
PR113.G4   1990
820.9′9287′09033—dc20   89–21449
                                                                CIP

*The authors gratefully acknowledge the generous support
of the Publications Committee of Simon Fraser
University.*

For Mary, Anne, Mary, and Laetitia

CONTENTS

ACKNOWLEDGMENTS

The four of us who wrote this book wish to thank each other for support, encouragement, and help that have ranged from the most concrete to the most intangible. Over the years, in a varying pattern of academic and personal relationships, we have exchanged cups of tea and occasional glasses of champagne, intellectual direction and redirection, references and books and photocopies and complaints and enthusiasms. Together we have tracked down elusive texts, coped with both antique typewriters and obstinate computers, and worked our way through all the other preliminaries of publishing. And we are still friends.

CONTRIBUTORS

ANN MESSENGER (Ph.D., Cornell University) is a Professor of English at Simon Fraser University. Her teaching and research center on the eighteenth century. She is the author of a book of essays comparing men and women writers, and is currently branching out into biographical work on women poets.

JEAN MALLINSON (Ph.D., Simon Fraser University) wrote her dissertation on contemporary Canadian women poets and how they used genre. She teaches English at a community college and has published poetry, short stories, and critical articles on Canadian women writers.

JULIET MCLAREN (Ph.D. candidate, Simon Fraser University) is writing her dissertation on postmodern Canadian poetry. Her scholarly interests range from the eighteenth through the twentieth centuries and include women's writing in all genres.

DIANA M. A. RELKE (Ph.D., Simon Fraser University) is a Canada Research Fellow and Assistant Professor of Interdisciplinary Studies at the University of Calgary. She is the author of several articles on poetry by Canadian women and is presently at work on a book-length comparative study of Australian and Canadian women writers.

INTRODUCTION

Women have been writers since the writing of literature began. Their numbers, few at first, grew dramatically in the seventeenth and eighteenth centuries, as literacy increased among the population in general and the female population in particular. As the readership—and market—grew, men and women not only went on producing the traditional genres but invented new ones, most notably the novel. In England, in the late seventeenth and eighteenth centuries, women and men together created the literary scene. Yet much of the women's writing fell into obscurity as time went on and is only now being recovered.

The purpose of these studies of four women writers is twofold: to continue the work of restoring to the light, or to brighter light, unjustly neglected women writers; and to contribute, both directly and indirectly, to the lively, on-going debate about the relationship of gender to discourse. The first of these purposes needs no explanation or justification; the value of such restoration work is now generally accepted. A few brief comments will clarify the second, that is, the nature of the debate and the part our studies have been designed to play in it.

The debate addresses two questions: Is the writing of the different genders different? and, if so, how? How does gender manifest itself, directly or indirectly, in literature?

The questions are not new, but they have not yet been fully explored. Although they were not of central concern to eighteenth-century commentators on literature, the observations of such commentators sometimes touch on the basic issue. For example, every critic who sneered at a poem because it was "by a Woman writt," to borrow Lady Winchilsea's phrase, [1] assumed that her gender had something to do with her discourse—in this case, rendering it inferior. When Mrs. Barbauld refused to collaborate with other women on a literary paper because "different sentiments and connections separate [literary women] much more than the joint interest of their sex would unite them,"[2] she assumed a discontinuity between gender and discourse.

Modern critics concern themselves with the questions in a number of ways. Although occasionally a critic will simply dismiss the idea that gender makes a difference in writing, most critics, especially feminists, take it seriously. Sometimes, like Annette Kolodny, they address the idea directly and attempt to test its validity. Generally, the conclusion is that gender does make a difference. Sometimes, like Sandra Gilbert and Susan Gubar, they assume that it does and proceed to analyze literature from that point of view. And sometimes, like Luce Irigaray, they apply the tools of theory to explore and articulate how it does, how gender informs discourse.[3] In none of our four studies here do we engage in such theoretical examination of the issue. Instead, we follow the other two paths; we both test and analyze. And we work by confronting our literary texts as directly as possible, by using, if we may be forgiven the slightly old-fashioned term, "practical criticism."

Chapter 1 is the test, and I conduct the test in practical terms. To examine the question of gender influence as objectively and fairly as possible, though always acknowledging that literary criticism is never scientifically pure, I needed to compare two poets, one male and one female. And I needed two poets whose lives and works, apart from their gender, had as many similarities as possible. I found the greatest number of similarities between two minor, pastoral poets who lived retired, private lives in the rural Midlands, two poets who were not only friends but mentor and protégée: William Shenstone (1714–1763) and Mary Whateley (later Mrs. Darwall) (1738–1825). Detailed comparisons of some of their work demonstrates beyond a doubt that, in this case at least, gender did make a difference—and shows something of what that difference was.

The rest of the book explores the work of three very different women who wrote in different genres and in radically different working conditions, women whose gender we found to be manifested in their work in a variety of ways. Their work is analyzed as poetry, as drama, and as autobiography—and as poetry, drama, and autobiography written by women. That is, the relationship of gender to discourse is addressed for the most part indirectly, in practice as it were, rather than directly as in chapter 1. My colleagues and I chose these particular authors not because they are representative of the women writers of the period—indeed they are not, since none of them is a novelist, none is a letter-writer—but because they illustrate the extremes, and the middle, of the economic class structure and of the working conditions that went along with economic class. Furthermore, they wrote in different genres, genres which range from the most public to the most private, from the most impersonal to the most personal (though these two pairs of opposites are not always synonymous). And we found that, despite the profound differences in the situations of these three writers and in the genres that they practiced, gender made a difference in every case.

Anne Finch, Countess of Winchilsea (1661–1720), the subject of chapter 2, had the easiest, most privileged life and hence the greatest freedom of all three authors from the constraints of being female. After her initial troubles—her exclusion from court after the Revolution of 1688—she settled happily in the country with a supportive husband and nephew, with a room of her own and no children to take up her time. She could publish or not as she chose, and for a long time she chose to publish very little. She could write anything she liked. She was free to express her gender or to ignore it if she could—but she could, or did, not, as Jean Mallinson's analysis shows. Her discussion of Anne Finch's best poetry, omitting her less interesting biblical paraphrases and religious verse and her plays, reveals that the poet was deeply concerned with genre and other literary conventions and with how she could adopt and adapt the forms available to her in order to express her own feminine perceptions.

Mary Pix (1666–1709), who never knew the security and freedom of an aristocratic country estate, was a middle-class woman who worked in the urban world of the commercial theater. Women were at a disadvantage in her world: although actresses could achieve positions of power in the theater, they were more often under the thumbs of the male actor-managers; women playwrights were generally treated by male playwrights as just more competition, and peculiarly undesirable competition, for the playgoers' shillings; and audiences tended to dismiss, or even hiss, women's plays. If, against all these odds, a woman did succeed as a playwright, her opportunities to express her ideas and her self were severely limited. Because drama is traditionally the most impersonal of genres, any direct self-expression is virtually impossible. And because to succeed a playwright had to cater for the most part to public taste, she could seldom risk challenging public opinion by expressing unorthodox ideas through her characters. But Mary Pix, as Juliet McLaren shows, not only succeeded in the competitive world of the theater, but also, in her comedies, managed against great odds to express her female concerns.

Laetitia Pilkington (1712–1750), at first a respectably married, middle-class woman like Mary Pix, soon sank to the lower fringes of the economic class structure to a life of poverty and insecurity—the direct opposite of Lady Winchilsea's position. Pilkington lived by her wits and her writing in a time when, on all levels but perhaps especially on the lower fringe, gender roles were inescapable. And she chose to write her autobiography, simultaneously the most personal and, because she published it, a highly public literary form. As the record of the life of a woman, her *Memoirs* inevitably evince her gender; she writes directly about herself as a dramatist can never do. Yet as Diana Relke's study shows, gender is manifested not only in the facts of Pilkington's life but also in other ways, including why and how she used the genre of autobiography. Gender here is style as well as substance.

Women were at work—and gender was at work—in eighteenth-century literature. In these four studies we have, to our own satisfaction at least, demonstrated that gender does play a role across a wide spectrum of the discourse of this century. It has been suggested that male and female utterance differed much less in the eighteenth than in the nineteenth century;[4] this may very well be true, but still, there are differences. We hope that our explorations of some of these differences will provide useful, practical material for the theoretical debate about the nature of the role that gender plays. To arrive at valid conclusions, the debate needs the broadest possible base of acquaintance with the women writers and the literature that they produced. Therefore we also hope— and this has been our deepest concern—that our book will further broaden that acquaintance: that it will help to restore, to the prominence in literary history that they deserve, four interesting and valuable women writers.

"Like—but oh, how different!":

WILLIAM SHENSTONE AND MARY WHATELEY DARWALL

ANN MESSENGER

John Langhorne had high praise for the tenderness and simplicity, and especially for the pastoral sensibilities, expressed in two of Dodsley's new publications of 1764. Reviewing *Original Poems on Several Occasions* "by Miss Whateley" in the *Monthly Review* for June, he heaped unqualified approval on the "pretty rural pieces," the "taste and candour," and the artistic skill he found in that slim volume, welcoming its author to the company of "the British Muses." Although he did preface his puff with two paragraphs defending the right of ladies to "amuse" themselves with writing poetry, especially elegies and pastorals, and recommending that "our fair Readers . . . express a charity of opinion" when ladies publish their work, his own high opinion of Mary Whateley's verse seems genuine rather than condescending or merely charitable.[1]

His opinion of the other book, *The Works in Verse and Prose of William Shenstone, Esq.*, is rather more mixed. In the May, 1764 issue of the *Monthly Review,* he had begun his review by quoting most of Dodsley's biographical preface to the book and some passages from Shenstone's own prefatory essay on elegy, adding only a few approving comments on the moral instruction contained in Shenstone's elegies and quoting from some of those poems (pp. 378–89). In June he concluded his review, praising the "Pastoral Ballad" and the lyrics, which took various forms, but deploring most of the songs and "Levities" and even some of the "Moral Pieces." He was still pleased with Shenstone's "valuable sentiments" and "easy and agreeable numbers," and he excused the publication of the inferior poetry by explaining that the book appeared posthumously. Dodsley, not Shenstone, he implied, was responsible for injudiciously allowing some of the pieces to see the light of day (pp. 450–63).

It may not be simply coincidental that Langhorne's review of Miss Whateley's book concludes and the second part of his review of Shenstone's begins on the same page of the June *Monthly*. He knew Miss Whateley—he had contributed an introductory poem to her book—and he knew that she had been Shenstone's protégée in the last few years before his death;[2] he mentions Shenstone's admiration of her poems. The language of the two reviews indicates that Langhorne perceived similarities in their poetry despite the difference in their sex, similarities especially in the lyric, pastoral, and elegiac modes: he praises both poets for tenderness of feeling, rural simplicity, and melody of verse.

Langhorne was not alone in associating these two poets. Ten years after their books appeared, in a work entitled *The Female Advocate; A Poem, Occasioned by Reading Mr. Duncombe's Feminead*, Mary Scott went so far as to call Miss Whateley "Daughter of SHENSTONE," calling particular attention to her as a pastoral poet:

> Daughter of SHENSTONE hail! hail charming maid,
> Well hath thy pen fair nature's charms display'd!
> The hill, the grove, the flow'r-enamell'd lawn,
> Shine in thy lays in brightest colours drawn:
> Nor be thy praise confin'd to rural themes,
> Or idly-musing Fancy's pleasing dreams;
> But still may contemplation (guest divine!)
> Expand thy breast, and prompt the flowing line.[3]

Mary Scott recognizes here the way pastoral description in Miss Whateley's poetry blends with ideas arising from contemplation of the landscape, the same blend that Shenstone's critics recognize in his verse.[4]

In fact, Shenstone and Miss Whateley had contemplated landscapes, literal and metaphorical, of considerable similarity. Both were children of the rural Midlands. Although Shenstone had spent some time in London, he passed most of his life in or near the Leasowes, his pretty little "farm" not far from Birmingham.[5] Although Mary Whateley lived for a while in Walsall, she grew up and wrote most of her early poetry in Beoley, a tiny village ten miles south of the Leasowes. The gentle countryside they celebrate in their poetry is much the same. Both were devoted to books. As a child, Shenstone apparently craved new books so much that he had to be lulled to sleep with a wooden substitute when an expected new book failed to arrive. As a girl, Mary did a great deal of reading despite the more traditional demands made upon her time by her needlework. She did not, of course, attend university as Shenstone did, but she acquired a literary education nonetheless. They liked the same poets, from Tibullus and Anacreon to Langhorne and Whitehead. They honored friendship as a virtue and cared deeply for their friends. Shenstone was particularly close to his fellow poets, Richard Graves, Richard Jago, and Thomas Percy; to his publisher, Robert Dodsley; and to Lady Luxborough. Miss Whateley's circle was smaller, but she had at least three close women friends, mentioned in her poems, the most intimate being Elizabeth Loggin, her vicar's daughter; she also had a number of male friends—all clerics except Shenstone—to whom she addressed poems. Both Shenstone and Miss Whateley were apparently content in Christian orthodoxy, though Miss Whateley expressed its doctrines more frequently and overtly in her poems than did her mentor. Christianity could not preserve them from occasional melancholy, however, a feeling they both expressed, sometimes as part of the convention of pastoral elegy, sometimes with evident sincerity. Perhaps their melancholy sprang partly from their appearance, for neither was physically attractive. Even Shenstone's best friends found him large, heavy, and coarse of form and face, with the added peculiarity of always wearing his own, prematurely gray, hair. Shenstone in turn found Miss Whateley "not handsome,"[6] a judgment with which she concurs in three of her own poems.[7] And both had come fairly young to the writing of verse. Shenstone wrote and published some poems while he was a student at Oxford, and though his collected poetry was not published until after his death, most of it had been composed before he was thirty-six. Miss Whateley's first book, the fruit of several years' work, was published when she was twenty-six.

Despite the difference of twenty-four years in their ages and despite their different gender, then, they had much in common. They shared, too, a general sense of the nature and purpose of poetry: that it should be moral in its content and didactic in its end, that it should be sincere but could sometimes be comic. Shenstone's range was wider; he wrote longer poems, imitated Spenser, tried a historical ballad or two, let himself go in humorous pieces that were occasionally vulgar. But his contemplative pastorals, especially his elegies, clearly fathered Mary Whateley's verses. She was perceived to be Shenstone's "daughter."

And yet, within these broad and general similarities, there are differences both subtle and profound. These differences are, I believe, explainable primarily by the different genders of the two poets. Feminist criticism often takes it for granted that gender difference explains artistic difference. It is useful to reexamine this assumption now and then, for gender can never be the whole explanation for artistic difference. Even in the case of William Shenstone and Mary Whateley, there were other significant differences, especially in temperament, Shenstone's being notoriously indolent and Miss Whateley's energetic.[8] But the similarities in their lives and work are so numerous and so striking that here it is possible to an unusual degree to conclude with validity that gender is a major cause of their differences.

To begin with one element in their poetics—their sense of the purpose of poetry. Shenstone articulated his sense of the ends that poetry serves, and how it best serves them, in prose essays, in verse itself, and in his letters. His most direct statement appears in "A Prefatory Essay on Elegy," written about 1744: "The most important end of all poetry is to encourage virtue. Epic and tragedy chiefly recommend the public virtues; elegy is of a species which illustrates and endears the private."[9] Poetry must be moral—"poetry without morality is but the blossom of a fruit-tree" (1:12)—and it should have the effect of making its readers virtuous, nourishing their moral characters as fruit nourishes their bodies. Shenstone can conceive of other reasons for publishing poetry: "Vanity and hunger" have often been a poet's true motives, he remarks sarcastically in his essay "On Publications" (2:4). However, first among "The most allowable reasons for appearing thus in public are . . . the advantage or amusement of our fellow-creatures" (2:4). The tones of these two essays differ considerably, the "Prefatory Essay" being a piece of academic analysis of the forms of poetry and "On Publications" primarily a satire on the vanity of bad poets. But in both Shenstone envisions poetry as an active force producing visible results in its readers. He does not speak overtly of the poet as an instructor, nor does he mention the usual Muse in these contexts.[10] Instead, the poet is identified with, subsumed in, the poetry, and as such is an active force for good.

Miss Whateley addresses the question of the purpose of poetry directly in "Elegy on the Uses of Poetry" (pp. 109–13) and indirectly in her Dedication. The "Elegy" is a pastoral meditation describing a quiet evening by the river, a time and place where Contemplation dwells, "Where Heav'n-born *Truth*, and keen-ey'd *Genius* rove, / Where *Peace* resides in *Freedom*'s Moss-roof'd Dome":

> *These* Heaven ordain'd the Guardians of the Muse;
>   Beneath their sacred Influence unconfin'd
> She soars, superior to terrestrial Views,
>   To harmonize, instruct, and charm Mankind.
>
> (p. 110)

The poem goes on to describe different kinds of poetry, kinds in which the Muse's "pleasing Task" is "To vindicate the Ways of God to Man" or "to sing of Swains and Flocks." Love is an allowed topic, but "licentious Freedom" is not; poets who debase the Muse by singing of vice or "venal *Flatt'ry*" deserve oblivion. The poet herself will praise only true merit and will never sink to evil themes. She concludes with thanks to the clergyman to whom the poem is addressed, thanks for his friendship and his verses, and with hopes that he will approve of hers.

It is the job of the Muse to "harmonize, instruct, and charm Mankind," not the purpose of the poet or of poetry itself. Miss Whateley has displaced the traditional and active function of instruction onto the figure of the Muse; Shenstone assumed that the poet / poem fulfilled that function. Of course, the Muse *is* poetry, but Miss Whateley's choice of the personification, a separate figure, seems significant. And even this separate figure is cautiously presented. Her main duties are traditionally feminine—to "harmonize" and "charm Mankind." Her duty to "instruct" is buried in the middle of the list. Furthermore, the bulk of this "Elegy" is taken up not with development of the idea of poetry-as-instruction but with rejection of immoral subject matter.[11] The poet is deeply concerned with the moral content of her poetry and the image of her own moral character embodied in the poetry. But, unlike the male poet, she does not claim the role of moral teacher for herself or for her poems.

Nor does she articulate the idea of poetry-as-instruction, as an active force, in her Dedication. She makes the usual modest statements that her poems were written simply for her own amusement, that they were not intended to be made public, and that they contain no novelties but only such humble themes "as Friendship, Gratitude, and native Freedom of Fancy, presented to my Thoughts" (p. 5). She does not grovel before her patroness, the Honorable Lady Wrottesley, nor abase herself as much as women writers were wont to do in their prefaces and dedications. She does go through the motions of modesty— but she does it with dignity. She even expresses confidence that her patroness "will find nothing in this little Collection to make you regret the Favour you have granted me of prefixing Your Name to it. My Pen was never prostituted to flatter a Friend or a Superior, or to revenge the Malevolence of an Enemy"— which accords with her standards as articulated in her "Elegy on the Uses of Poetry." She goes on to complete the description of herself as a poet: "These I thought Views below the Dignity of a Pen consecrated to Truth and Virtue; from which, I hope, I may say, without Vanity, mine has never deviated" (pp. 8–9). She does not speak of her poetry as teaching truth—as, in Shenstone's words, designed to "encourage" or "recommend" virtue. She speaks instead of her own moral character as a poet, of her pen's dedication to truth and virtue.

Miss Whateley *expresses* truth, virtue, morality in her poetry, but she does not take upon herself the active role of teacher, of inculcator of truth, virtue, morality. Shenstone does. In so doing, he is entirely conventional: that the purpose of poetry was to instruct was an accepted truth. He defines that purpose further by specifying that his poems will instruct his readers in the virtues. He takes on a particular version of the usual public role. Miss Whateley's role is private: she will be, not do. Her poems are not purely passive: some are designed to "transmit" her "Friendship, Gratitude, and Regard" to her friends (p. 7). But that too is a relatively private function. And in a poem transmitting gratitude to a fellow poet for his praise, she speaks of him as a teacher and of herself as improved by his moral lessons. [12] However seriously she took herself as a poet and however deeply she yearned for fame (and her Dedication and some of her poems hint at both), as a woman poet she did not assume the authority of a teacher. Gender made a difference.

Shenstone says much more about the purpose of poetry than Miss Whateley does; he was, in a sense, a professional man of letters. His professionalism also appears as he addresses other elements in poetics. In his essays, he discusses many technical matters, including alliteration, rhyme, and prosody, the evils of too great regularity, and the need for heightened language in odes (2:176, 179–81, 271). In his first pastoral elegy and elsewhere he insists that sincerity is the first criterion in poetry and that simplicity is superior to art. Poetry should accomplish its ends by affecting the passions (2:176); indeed, the "voice of Sentiment" is the only voice which can "strike the Passions, which is the only Merit of Poetry." [13] Miss Whateley, with her stated commitment to truth, clearly agreed with the criterion of sincerity, a growing desideratum in the mid-eighteenth century. [14] But she said nothing in print about the technical criteria or other elements that Shenstone addresses; that is, she did not appear publicly as a professional poet.

Both Shenstone and Miss Whateley were professional about their poetry, but only he wrote in any detail about that profession. Both, however, wrote about the dangers of possessing the gift of poetry, Shenstone in a rather strange poem ostensibly lamenting Pope's death, Miss Whateley in one of her strongest poems, "The Power of Destiny." The idea of danger was traditional. Miss Whateley herself mentions elsewhere "the rapturous Flame, which pains the Breast / With Extasies too strong" (p. 90). But their handling of it was quite different.

Shenstone's Elegy 8 is subtitled "He describes his early love of poetry, and its consequences"; the poem is dated 1745 and a footnote calls attention to the fact that it was "Written after the death of Mr. Pope" (1:31). The poem says nothing directly about Pope but it says a great deal about the painful consequences for Shenstone of possessing the poetic gift, especially poverty (the swain's fold grows thinner) and an inflated sense of his own abilities. Indeed, he blames his friends, especially Graves, for praising and encouraging him, though he welcomes and blesses "such error." His friends, poets themselves, should have known better. The mixture of tones here is disconcerting, to say the least. Then, with a simile about Phoebus and Venus, he makes a transition (which does not really work) to "Twitnam's widow'd bow'r" where the Muses droop and Elegy forms a dark garland—for Pope, though he is not named. But, in his role as a satirist, he is alluded to:

> Enough of tears has wept the virtuous dead;
>   Ah might we now the pious rage controul!
> Hush'd be my grief ere ev'ry smile be fled,
>   Ere the deep swelling sigh subvert the soul!

In tribute to the laughter, however grim, of Pope's satires, Shenstone will try to smile despite his grief. The stanza is not entirely clear (whose is the "pious rage"? Pope's or Shenstone's?) and Shenstone is more concerned to express his own reaction to Pope's death than to say much about Pope. But he has understood Pope's spirit.

The next and final stanza, in a manner untypically indirect, returns to the idea of the dangers of possessing the poetic gift:

> If near some trophy spring a stripling bay,
>   Pleas'd we behold the graceful umbrage rise;
> But soon too deep it works its baneful way,
>   And, low on earth, the prostrate ruin lies.

To make sure the reader understands, Shenstone (or perhaps Dodsley) added the following footnote: "Alludes to what is reported of the bay tree, that if it is planted too near the walls of an edifice, its roots will work their way underneath, till they destroy the foundation" (1:33). The bay tree, the poetic gift, undermined Pope's fragile "edifice," and he died at fifty-six after nearly a lifetime of ill health. Shenstone too was frequently unwell, despite his bulky body and his mineral springs at the Leasowes. In poems and letters he speaks repeatedly of illnesses ranging from the obviously hypochondriacal to the genuine. So, while the first half of the elegy is overtly devoted to his own financial and emotional suffering, in this final stanza he seems to be associating himself with Pope physically, as a fellow bard threatened with dissolution by the power of the poetic gift within. He flattered himself.

Mary Whateley too alludes to Pope in her poem on this theme, "The Power of Destiny," which stands in first place in her book (pp. 13–16). In heroic couplets, one of her favorite meters (though Shenstone, her mentor, only used them once in a serious poem and often found their effects undesirable [1:22]), she speculates about the "malignant" source of her gift and imagines how she would have behaved as a poet if she had been a man. Pope, in "An Epistle to Dr. Arbuthnot," had also speculated about the source of his gift:

> Why did I write? what sin to me unknown
> Dipt me in Ink, my Parents', or my own?
>   (ll. 125–26)

Miss Whateley does not halfway blame her parents, as Pope does, but blames only the "malignant Star" that made her "dip in Ink, / And write in Rhyme before I knew to think"—another connection with Pope, who "lisp'd in Numbers" (l. 128). If "Fate, propitious to [her] Wish," had made her a man, she would still have been a poet, and would have neglected whatever profession she was educated to follow—divinity, medicine, or law. Pope, on the other hand, is careful to establish that he "left no Calling for this idle Trade, / No Duty broke, no Father dis-obey'd" (ll. 129–30). He is busy creating a high moral character for himself in the "Epistle," while Miss Whateley emphasizes her rebelliousness. And yet the rebelliousness is not literally hers—she is not a man and has no profession to rebel against. In this poem, she can describe the disturbing power of her gift only indirectly.

She concludes with what looks like a sly dig at Shenstone and his frequent laments, as in Elegy 8, about his poverty:

> In short, whatever my Employ had been,
> It soon had yielded to this darling *Sin*:
> And nought but *Russel*'s Land, or *Gideon*'s Purse,
> Had sav'd the Poet—from—the Poet's Curse.

But is it only poverty that is "the Poet's Curse"? In the immediate context here, yes. But more generally, looking back over the poem as a whole, the poet's curse is the gift of poetry itself, making the clergyman, the doctor, and the lawyer—when they would rather be poets—miserable in their professions. And the woman poet, who, like Pope, had no profession but had a gift bestowed by a "malignant Star," feels similarly cursed.

But the gift could sometimes be a pleasure. Both Shenstone and Miss Whateley had a sense of humor, which lightens and brightens some of their verse. Shenstone has a whole group of "Levities" in his book, deplored by his early reviewers but appreciated by some of his modern readers. [15] He could even make fun of his own poverty and vanity, the disadvantages he groaned about in Elegy 8. "The Poet and the Dun," in comic anapests, describes the visit of a bill collector and the poet's desperate attempt to think of a way to earn some money—as "shoe-boy, or courtier, or pimp, or procurer" (1:226). But a letter arrives, full of praise for his poetry, so he scribbles all night—until the bill collector arrives again in the morning. He concludes, " 'Ah! friend, 'tis but idle to make such a pother, / Fate, fate has ordain'd us to plague one another' " (1:227). His problems are not solved, but his verse about them is a delight.

Miss Whateley used the same meter in the one comic poem in her book, "To Mr. O——y, Upon his asking the Author to paint his Character" (pp. 62–63). In spite of the name in the title, I believe this poem was requested by and addressed to Shenstone.[16] It is both lively and diplomatic, both teasing and flattering. Shenstone chose only this one of Mary Whateley's poems to include in his Miscellany; he must have liked the image of himself it presented:

> Shou'd I blend in one Piece of superlative Merit,
> Good-nature and Wit, Condescension and Spirit;
> Shou'd with Modesty, Ease and Politeness be join'd;
> Unlimited Freedom, with Manners refined;

and so on. The poem also bears witness to his value as a model, and to Miss Whateley's grace in the role of protégée.

Shenstone and Miss Whateley shared other genres besides that of anapestic comic verse. Both wrote songs; Shenstone has eighteen poems so labeled and his protégée two. Shenstone conceived of the song as a very minor genre indeed, as a kind of poetry in which "flimziness" is required (2:173, 178). His own songs live up to that requirement. They are graceful performances, full of Daphnes and Damons and Delias doing their usual thing. But except for one mention of British youth as being "free-born" (1:151), which is of a piece with his patriotic sentiments expressed elsewhere, his songs *say* nothing at all. Miss Whateley's say just a fraction more than nothing at all. In the flimsiest, Sylvia laments Damon's unfaithfulness and warns other maidens to beware of love's eloquence (pp. 60–61). Perhaps one can sense a little more than mere convention here, knowing that the author is a woman and that Shenstone required real passion in love poetry. But the poem has nothing of the obvious depth of feeling visible in Anne Killigrew's second "Pastoral Dialogue" when her unhappy shepherdess prays to Heaven, "My flocks from Wolves, my Heart from Love, defend."[17] In her other song (pp. 42–44), Miss Whateley does introduce a modicum of moral content, though no other depth of feeling or meaning. Using an apparently male speaker (the only time she does so), she addresses "dear *Pastora*," inviting her to enjoy the evening hour "In yonder artless Maple Bow'r, / With blooming Woodbines twin'd." The speaker begs Pastora to listen to his vows and swears that he is sincere. Every shepherd says that, but this one attributes his truthfulness to his rural character, for "Truth [is] scarce known among the Great"; "On Pride's false Glare I look with Scorn," he adds, and he assumes that his equally rural Pastora is similarly upright. He concludes:

> The Lily fades, the Rose grows faint,
>   Their transient Bloom is vain;
> But lasting Truth and Virtue paint
>   *Pastora* of the Plain.

The two ideas expressed here are commonplaces: that beauty, both human and floral, fades, and that moral character is the best cosmetic. The combining of the ideas in this fashion is less common, and their presence gives the song a little substance. But Miss Whateley did not spend much time writing songs. A woman's pen "consecrated to Truth and Virtue" had better things to do than go on creating "flimziness."

One of those other activities was imitating ancient models. Miss Whateley wrote three such poems, Shenstone one. His "Anacreontic" (1:143–44), a free adaptation of Anacreon's sixth ode, describes a sleeping Cupid discovered by a Muse who, concerned about the sorrows he inflicts on the world, steals his arrows and throws them in the "Castalian fount." The poet predicts that Cupid will soon find the arrows again and that their power will be redoubled because they were "Dipt in the muse's mystic spring," a nice tribute to the efficacy of poetry. Miss Whateley's imitation of the third book of Tibullus (pp. 39–41) is less free. She changes the speaker in the poem, a lovelorn shepherd, to a shepherdess, and adds the idea that the speaker is a poet, but the poem as a whole, with updated allusions, tells the same story: the speaker rejects all forms of gratification except love, and if she cannot have that, would choose to die.

Her two Anacreontics are freer imitations and more interesting poems. Both are adaptations of the twenty-third ode in which Anacreon's lyre remains silent when he wishes to sing of heroic deeds and will only perform when his topic is love. Miss Whateley's poems follow the same outline but supply much more detail, not only updated allusions but also a speaking role for the lyre. In the first (pp. 21–22),[18] she replaces Cadmus and Hercules with "mighty *Fred'rick*," whose "Fame / Inspires my Breast with martial Flame." When she attempts to sing his praises, however, her lyre replies, " 'What have I with War to do? / Love, my Lays belong to you.' " She returns to the heroic topic in more detail, citing Frederick's great victory at Zorndorf (in August, 1758) and mentioning Dohna and Seidlitz, who helped him win the battle. However, these must "yield / To *Venus,* and her *Paphian Field,*" because her lyre will not cooperate. Defeated, she turns graciously to Venus with the conclusion, "Love and *Verse* can conquer Steel." This poem is unusual in its specific allusions to current historical events. Miss Whateley was, as Langhorne and Mary Scott described her, a lady pastoral poet; most of the time she remained in that role, which did not include commenting on political events. And even here she keeps up the role by using a kind of apophasis, by saying that her lyre will *not* sing about what she is describing. In the second version of the same Anacreontic (pp. 84–85), her political content is generalized to commendation of "*Brunswick*" and "*Britannia*'s Thunders," but her lyre still refuses to cooperate, this time with a more direct reprimand:

"Murd'ring Steel and dreadful Wounds,
Heroes bleeding, Heaps of Slain,
Strew'd promiscuous o'er the Plain;
Foaming Billows, Seas on fire,
Ill become a Virgin's Lyre."

The lyre's message is plain: ladies do not write about such things. "Convinc'd, asham'd," she returns to her "Painted Meadows, purling Streams," and concludes again that love is stronger than Mars.

Only once more did Miss Whateley mention matters political in her poems: in the "Hymn to Solitude" she rejoices that "A *British Brunswick* reigns," which makes possible her safety and peace (p. 52). Shenstone, and other male pastoral poets, commonly use their poetry to express general or specific political stances. Sometimes their remarks are just vaguely patriotic, like Miss Whateley's about *"British Brunswick,"* but sometimes they tackle particular issues.[19] For instance, in his elegies Shenstone speaks out strongly against the slave trade (Elegy 20) and for the protection of the English woollen manufacture and trade (10, 18, and elsewhere). One of his long "Moral Pieces," "The Ruin'd Abby; or, The Effects of Superstition" (1:308–21), surveys much of English history and proclaims England's superiority to Catholic countries. Even one of his flimsy songs lauds "free-born" British youth, as I mentioned before. But Miss Whateley's lyre had instructed her that political happenings were not proper material for a lady poet, and, for the most part, she heeded its lesson.

The pastoral mode, on the other hand, was proper. Fortunately, it was a fairly accommodating mode, and Miss Whateley used it to varying extents in each poem in her 1764 volume except "To Mr. O——y." She even used it when she undertook philosophical argument modeled on Pope's *Essay on Man;* in "Occasion'd by reading some Sceptical Essays," wrong thinking is defeated by "the vernal Rose" and "the Woodbine's od'rous Soul" (p. 54). The pastoral mode dominates Shenstone's poetry as well, no matter what his subject matter. Catholic superstition or the moral choice between Sloth and Virtue (a revealing variation on the usual Pleasure / Virtue topos), the sorrow of the imprisoned Princess Elizabeth or the eccentricities of the village schoolmistress—all are couched in pastoral terms. For Shenstone and Miss Whateley, the language of poetry was the language of hill and grove, tree and leaf, nymph and swain.

On rare occasions they combined the pastoral mode with satire. Shenstone rhapsodized about the young poet's need for thrift in "Oeconomy," a satiric "Moral Piece" in which gold, "Lovely, as when th' Hesperian fruitage smil'd / Amid the verd'rous grove," proves unattainable (1:289). With her usual pastoral imagery, Miss Whateley, like many other women poets, satirized foolish women:

How various is the Female Mind!
As with the softest Breeze of Wind
   The trembling Osiers move;
So, as capricious *Fancy* reigns,
We sigh in Health, we smile at Pains,
   Admire, despise, and love.

                        (p. 26)

But neither Shenstone nor Miss Whateley was primarily a satirist. Both habitually used pastoral rather than satire to "encourage" or express the virtues.

They were alike in their use of forms of poetry as well as modes. Besides comic anapests, songs, and imitations, described above, they both wrote odes, verse letters, and occasional poems. And for both, the pastoral elegy was a major genre.

Shenstone took the pastoral elegy seriously. He devoted his "Prefatory Essay" to that form and wrote twenty-six of them. Mary Whateley wrote seven, one being her imitation of Tibullus. All of Shenstone's are in iambic pentameter quatrains with alternate rhyme, a form he defends in the "Prefatory Essay"; Miss Whateley broke the rules and wrote two of hers in heroic couplets, but the others conform. All the elegies by both poets are in large measure pastoral and for the most part melancholy in tone, as the genre requires. Both write about friendship and death, poetry and gardens, love and the place where happiness is to be found. But there are differences.

When Miss Whateley writes about death in "Elegy on a much lamented Friend" (pp. 23–25), she leans heavily on the pathetic fallacy in the first half of the poem but then turns to specific details of her friend's unhappy life: fortune had been adverse, malice and envy had pursued her, a friend had loved her but a fool had scorned her. She concludes with the idea of death as inevitable and as a leveler: her friend will join Newton, Lely, Thomson, Handel, and Milton "in Shade impervious," and she herself will eventually join her friend. Both form and ideas are conventional but the combination of elements in the poem is interestingly suggestive—was the dead friend an artist of some sort? Was the scornful fool a lover contemptuous of the lady's talents? We cannot know. But we can admire the way convention is made to suggest these possibilities and the way the deep and dignified feeling comes through.

When Shenstone wrote about death in Elegy 3 (1:18–20), he described a poet's death, outlining his virtues in a fairly general fashion and giving a great deal of emphasis to the dead poet's lack of money. "He little knew the sly penurious art"; the "sons of wealth" failed to protect him; "He wish'd for wealth, for much he wish'd to give." Only "peasant hands" performed his last rites, while "pow'r and wealth's unvarying cheek was dry!" Perhaps the dead poet is indirectly Shenstone himself; he makes the same complaints about money directly in many other poems. In any case, the main focus of the lament is on the conditions surrounding the poet's death. The life and character of the dead poet are not visible through the veils of convention. Miss Whateley's poem was more personal. On another occasion Shenstone used the subject of death quite unconventionally. In Elegy 22 (1:81–84), he imagines himself about to fall asleep when the specter of his dead love, Silvia, rises before him to describe her death and to complain that body-snatchers have robbed her grave. The subtitle of the poem makes it clear that this is not merely Gothic fantasy but a real social concern of the day: "Written in the year——when the rights of sepulture were so frequently violated." One cannot expect personal feeling in such a poem and there is none. Instead, there is the oddity of Gothic narrative used to address a public issue. Miss Whateley seldom addresses public issues, and never in her elegies.

Both Shenstone and Miss Whateley felt, as all pastoral poets do, that the public world—the world of the city and of public affairs—was in various ways less desirable than the retirement of the countryside. Both address the theme directly on many occasions, and it forms a backdrop to their work as a whole. Shenstone's feelings about rural retirement tend to be mixed, however. In his seventh pastoral elegy, for example, he bemoans his loneliness and describes a rather unpleasant rural scene which includes an uncomfortable storm; the ghost of Wolsey arises to tell him that he can show him the way to the brighter scene of the city and the "paths of pow'r"—which inevitably entail all kinds of corruption, falsehood, and impiety. So, despite his longing for "social joys," the pastoral poet rejects Wolsey's offer in favor of piety, friendship, all the other rural virtues, and the loneliness of the country (1:27–30). Many other poems are similarly ambivalent. The twenty-fourth pastoral elegy on the imprisonment of Eleanor of Bretagne uses the historical material specifically "to suggest the imperfect pleasures of a solitary life" (1:90). "A Pastoral Ode to the Honourable Sir Richard Lyttleton" (1:174–81) laments at length the loneliness of the countryside and its lack of opportunity for fame, but accept its beauties and pleasures joyfully—when various rich and titled friends come to visit. Shenstone always concludes in favor of the country as the pastoral convention requires, but his own ambivalence tends to undermine that convention. Perhaps this is why his Victorian editor, the Reverend George Gilfillan, found his poems insincere.[20] A more recent critic, A. R. Humphreys, was closer to the mark when he compared Shenstone's attitude to Touchstone's on life in the Forest of Arden: "In respect that it is solitary, I like it very well; but in respect that it is private, it is a very vile life. Now in respect that it is in the fields, it pleaseth me well; but in respect it is not in the court, it is tedious" (*As You Like It,* III.ii.15–18).[21] The Fool is challenging the pastoral convention in his own indirectly direct manner; Shenstone uses the convention but weakens it with his own ambivalence.

Whatever Miss Whateley might have felt about the limitations of the pastoral conventions in poetry, she expressed no ambivalence toward the country itself. Her poems express no boredom with retirement, no longing for the busier scenes of the world. She celebrates the beauties of hill and river, tree and blossom, and courts the solitude and quiet of an evening alone in the garden. When she must leave her country home for the city, she looks forward with distress to the "Crowds and Noise" she will find there and concludes that she will be unable to write in such surroundings.[22] Though she does once mention Birmingham as a place "Where Treasure flows, and useful Arts increase" (p. 30), that is the only kind word she has for the urban world.

I think her love for the country was genuine. Like Shenstone, she wanted both fame and human companionship, but unlike Shenstone, her love for the country was not spoiled by the feeling that friends and fame were hard to come by there. Friends she had in her country village, not rich and titled but apparently satisfactory. Fame was another matter. As a woman, she knew she could not expect much, and that little could be most gracefully obtained by staying put in her country village while her male friends, including Shenstone himself, brought her work to the notice of the world. Especially as a young unmarried woman, she would have risked soiling her reputation if she had sought the "paths of pow'r" that Shenstone halfway craved. Home was safe. So, most of the time, she stayed there, and she wrote about its rural beauties with unambivalent love.

She seems to have been aware of Shenstone's ambivalence, including his genuine love for his own piece of the country, his pretty Leasowes. Her "Elegy written in a Garden" (pp. 56–59) was quite clearly written in and about his garden, and she knew that nothing made him happier than to hear it praised. She admires the "mingled Beauties" and "varied Prospects" that Shenstone had worked so hard to create; she recognizes that "Here polish'd *Art* assumes fair *Nature*'s Face," the exact balance that he wanted to achieve. She knows that a pastoral elegy must "encourage virtue," so she notices a gaudy insect, compares it to "the gay *Belinda*" who is being frivolous in the city, and sends it to her as a warning to mend her ways. She expresses her own content with health (instead of beauty) and an ivy wreath mixed with field flowers (instead of bay), and concludes modestly that she is

> Pleas'd, while this artless rural Verse I raise,
> To see superior Merit shine confest;

> Supremely happy when my humble Praise
> Can give one Transport to the gen'rous Breast.

Shenstone, in his double role as landscape gardener and literary mentor, and rather short of "Transports," must have been pleased as well.

Miss Whateley does not undermine her pastoral poems with ambivalence toward retirement in the country as Shenstone does. Perhaps she was more tightly bound by the pastoral convention than he; perhaps she was more simply sincere; perhaps she was a better poet. But, like Shenstone, she does use the pastoral elegy to express personal unhappiness. Her unhappiness is a profound agony of spirit. His is merely self-pity.

Shenstone's self-pity often centers on money. Despite his frequent rejections of wealth in favor of friendship and other virtues, rejections dictated by the pastoral convention, he complains just as frequently that he needs money in order to be as benevolent as he would like or in order to give Delia the gifts that will win her from a richer swain. The ninth pastoral elegy "describes his disinterestedness" while the tenth repines at the dispensations of Fortune. In the seventeenth, he regrets that his poverty is as dire as that of Marius, but in the nineteenth, he claims his "breast [is] unsully'd by the lust of gold" (1:69). And so it goes. Small wonder that Reverend Gilfillan found him insincere. Miss Whateley, on the other hand, seldom mentions money in her 1764 collection, and when she does, it is rejected as irrelevant to happiness and inimical to virtue. As a young, unmarried gentlewoman living at home, she had no chance to earn or control money anyway, no small income to apportion and deplore as Shenstone did. There was nothing to interfere with the high-minded rejection of filthy lucre required by the pastoral convention.

Shenstone's self-pity sprang from other sources as well. Ill health and boredom, loneliness and spleen, winter weather and disappointed love appear regularly in his poems. And despite his real talent for friendship, he complains in Elegy 13 of a coolness arising between himself and a friend; he threatens that his health, already poor, will decline, he will die, and *then* the unfaithful friend will be sorry! Pastoral elegies were supposed to be melancholy, according to Shenstone's own prescription, and he certainly took advantage of that convention to express what can only be described as self-pity.

Miss Whateley's pastoral elegies are less consistently melancholy. In them, she mourned the death of a friend and said goodbye to the countryside with suitable grief, but she admired Shenstone's garden and discussed the uses of poetry in more cheerful tones. Her subject matter sometimes overrode the convention. She seems to have possessed a less morose temperament as well. But on one occasion she uses the pastoral elegy to express something beyond moroseness, beyond melancholy, beyond self-pity—something that can only be described as agonized despair.

"Liberty, an Elegy . . . Feigned to be written from the happy Valley of Ambara" is the second poem in her 1764 collection (pp. 17–20). It is addressed to her closest friend, Elizabeth Loggin, and describes the wretchedness of imprisonment. The poet, "Myra," is trapped like Rasselas in a supposedly happy valley where nothing is lacking except freedom. Miss Whateley echoes Johnson's language as well as his story as she describes the marble palaces and velvet lawns and endless entertainments with which the royal Abyssinian children pass the time. Myra, like Rasselas, is profoundly unhappy in the valley. "With Pleasure cloy'd, and sick of tasteless Ease," her "boundless Mind" is ever unsatisfied. She craves variety, freedom, something beyond the sweetness of the valley. But she is trapped: "Here wretched *Myra*'s destin'd to remain."

This devotion to the idea of freedom received high praise in the *Critical Review,* which compared Miss Whateley to Mrs. Macaulay and "many of our fair countrywomen" who were engaged in the struggle for liberty.[23] Shenstone too must have approved, since he praises British freedom now and then in his own pages. But the liberty Miss Whateley is talking about here is something other than political.

I read this poem as allegory. Shenstone probably did not. Indeed, he disapproved of that mode. In one of his essays, he said so directly: "I think nothing truly poetic, at least no poetry worth composing, that does not strongly affect one's passions: and this is but slenderly effected by fables, allegories, and lies" (2:176). And, as a man, he had no need of the protective veil of allegory. Miss Whateley, "daughter of Shenstone," did not normally use allegory. Her love poems could be allegories of her own experiences and feelings, but they could also be purely conventional. One cannot say. But in a single case, the case of "Liberty," I think one can say. Here, as a woman, she needed and used the veil.

"Myra" (an anagram of "Mary") is trapped in the fictional world of pastoral poetry, a world as fictional as Rasselas's happy valley. She is so entirely surrounded by the conventions of murmuring streams and warbling birds that "Harmony grows Discord to [her] Ear." She longs to get out into a world closer to reality, a world not merely pretty; she wants "To range the *Sun-burnt* Hill, the *rifted* Grove" (my italics). But ladies were not supposed to write about anything but prettiness. Her own lyre had told her so quite clearly in her Anacreontics. The allegorical reading of "Liberty" is further supported by the fact that in her book she placed it right after "The Power of Destiny," a poem which concluded that the poet's gift was "the Poet's Curse." The themes of the two poems connect; "wretched *Myra*" suffers from that curse because she feels destined to remain a pastoral poet until she dies. And her wretchedness is so extreme and is caused by such an improper rebelliousness, that she can speak of it only under the nearly impenetrable veil of allegory.[24]

But "Myra" escaped from the happy valley—to some extent. Much in her life and in the world around her had changed before she published her second collection of poems in 1794. Shenstone had died. Tastes in poetry had altered somewhat. Women writers were becoming more acceptable, especially virtuous women writers.[25] Miss Whateley's first book had been praised in the *Reviews.* And Miss Whateley herself had married the Reverend John Darwall, produced six children, been widowed, and gone to live in Wales.

Her second book, *Poems on Several Occasions* (Walsall, 1794; two volumes), reflects the greater breadth of her experience. She still writes many pastorals, and, however morally instructive her poems may be, she still lays no claim to the role of teacher that Shenstone had automatically taken on. But she tackles a wider range of forms, including a pastoral drama, a number of sonnets, and a piece of Ossianic poetic prose. She occasionally addresses public, even political, topics, as when she praises General Elliott in her ode on the peace treaty of January 1783. She performs public functions when she writes hymns for her husband's congregation to sing and epilogues for actresses to deliver from the stage on special occasions. She expresses a warm patriotism. She longs comically but honestly for money in a wonderful "Hymn to Plutus," in which she recognizes that money brings liberty and that most people do not ask how one's money was obtained. (This poem looks like a dig at Shenstone's hypocrisy about money.) She defends the strength of women's friendships and the uprightness of women's characters. And the only cry of anguish comparable to that in "Liberty" comes from a Scottish male persona who had the bad luck to fall in love with his highborn master's daughter; even though he is a minstrel, he is not an allegorical representation of Mary Darwall.

Clearly, Mrs. Darwall was a less restricted person than Miss Whateley had been. She still flicks a light satiric lash at silly women as she had done before, but now she flicks it at silly men as well. She mentions herself as a poet more often. She uses a kind of apophasis again—but not to conceal her wish to write about heroic themes; this time she uses it when she claims that she is unable to write pastoral—and follows that claim with "Valentine's Day," a pastoral drama that is thirty-five pages long. Clearly, her sense of humor was still alive and well. She uses no allegory to conceal herself as a poet. Instead, when she describes the transplanting of a bay tree to a warmer spot where it will grow better in better soil, she turns the potential allegory into a transparent metaphor by exclaiming, "O! might such blessings crown thy planter's toil" (2:105). She no longer needs to hide. The poet's gift is no longer the poet's curse.

In my chapter title I quote Wordsworth:

> Yes, it was the mountain Echo,
> Solitary, clear, profound,
> Answering to the shouting Cuckoo,
> Giving to her sound for sound!
>
> Unsolicited reply
> To a babbling wanderer sent;
> Like her ordinary cry,
> Like—but oh, how different!

For Wordsworth, Echo is superior to the Cuckoo; he goes on to describe her as providing intimations of immortality. Mary Whateley Darwall was perceived as echoing Shenstone, at least in her first book, and for me, she, like Wordsworth's Echo, is superior to her original. Such a judgment is, of course, highly subjective. But when she is at her best, her poems have, I believe, far more strength and energy and solidity than Shenstone's. She is sometimes platitudinous, sometimes, to a modern ear, unpleasantly pious and moralistic. But she is more often interesting, even exciting, as she pours all her force, all her self, into building an identity in her poetry. Writing poetry was not just an exercise, as it was so often for Shenstone. It was an outlet, her only outlet. He had, besides poetry, his Leasowes and his letters, his collection of prints and his books. He had, within the constraints of his income, his masculine freedom. Miss Whateley, before she married, had only her poetry, and it was often better than her mentor's.

It is impossible to establish differences in the quality of poetry to the satisfaction of all readers. But differences—and likenesses—of other elements in two bodies of work can be addressed, and in the case of William Shenstone and Mary Whateley Darwall, the differences I think are clearly due in large measure to their different gender.

One final point has to do with differences not just between the two poets but also between Miss Whateley's and Mrs. Darwall's poems. I have sketched only briefly the differences between her two collections, but enough, I hope, to suggest the nature of the changes. The changes are due partly, of course, to her increased experience of life. But she had not been a cloistered maiden; even before she published her 1764 collection, she had lived for about three and a half years in the growing town of Walsall looking after the household of her brother, who was a busy attorney. Yet she barely mentions this wider world in her first book. But when she married, her status changed. The wife and then widow of a vicar, a respected mother and stepmother, was less vulnerable than a young spinster; she could and did write more freely. Anne Finch, writing at a time when women writers were less welcome, behaved similarly, though even more circumspectly. As Miss Kingsmill, she kept her talent totally hidden; as Mrs. Finch, she allowed a few poems to get into print and some others to circulate among friends; as Lady Winchilsea, she published a book.[26] For Mrs. Darwall, too, her status, specifically her marital status, affected her poetry. Shenstone's marital status—he was a bachelor—had nothing to do with his. Gender made the difference.

ANNE FINCH: A WOMAN POET AND THE TRADITION

JEAN MALLINSON

Anne Finch, Countess of Winchilsea, poet and gentlewoman, never completely disappeared from the tradition of literary commentary which keeps texts alive and draws readers to them. Wordsworth admired her and recorded his admiration in published prose and private letters; Virginia Woolf wrote feelingly about her in *A Room of One's Own;* Myra Reynolds's 1903 edition of her work made her poems available.[1] Yet this edition was not reprinted until 1974, and, except for a few poems and fragments of poems which have appeared in anthologies, her work is not widely known, and has been little studied. It has not become part of what Frank Kermode calls "the secular canon; that is, it has not been guaranteed to be of such value that . . . exegesis is justified without argument. . . . "[2] Yet, without making extravagant claims for the value of her work, it is possible to justify exegesis of it on the grounds both of its intrinsic interest and its place in the tradition of women's poetry which scholarship and commentary are now engaged in establishing.

Myra Reynolds, in her introduction to the *Poems,* correctly judges Anne Finch to be a minor poet and rightly credits her with the versatility typical of the great writers of her age. She wrote "in all the popular literary forms except comedy. Love songs, sacred songs, pindarics, satires, epistles, fables, translations, tragedies, verse criticism, and one prose critical essay. . . . "(p. xvii). These genres were given her by the literature of her time, but the ways in which she adapted, modified, embellished, and sometimes transformed the conventions of genre can be illuminated by reading her poems as texts written by a woman.[3]

Paul Fussell has said of the making of literature that it is "a matter of the engagement of a vulnerable self with a fairly rigid coded medium so tough that it bends and alters only under the most rigorous pressure, pressure which only the rarest spirits among writers can exert."[4] As a woman writing in the late seventeenth century, Anne Finch was exceptionally vulnerable, yet she still managed to leave her distinctive mark on some of the genres she essayed, to bend the coded medium.

A striking instance of the difference made by gender in the handling of a literary convention is provided by Anne Finch's introductions and prologues to her poetry. This small genre offers a good starting point for commentary because her poems in this kind can be set beside similar pieces written by women poets who were almost her contemporaries. Looked at together, these poems provide a kind of composite picture of the woman poet's images of both her plight and her strengths. Such a picture presents a microcosm of the woman poet's sense of herself as a poet, a sense which is elaborated in the macrocosm of poetry which she makes.

The set piece in which an author apologizes for his poems is a very old convention, and there is in seventeenth-century occasional verse a marked strain of self-deprecation, but the prologues and introductions which women poets of that time wrote have a sexual resonance which is unmistakable. The apologia has always been double-edged—used to establish both authority and seemly humility. A woman poet writing in this mode typically extends the convention to include a statement about the territory to which she feels she can, as a woman, legitimately lay claim; her perceived entitlement is usually modest. Her authority is often established through a naming of literary models or precedents. Anne Bradstreet's *The Tenth Muse Lately Sprung up in America,* published in London in 1650, contains a "Prologue" in this vein. In her opening lines, she eschews heroic matter—"To sing of Wars, of Captains, and of Kings, / Of Cities founded, Common-wealths begun"—as "too superiour things" for her "mean pen."[5] Her "obscure Lines" would only "dim their worth." She invokes Bartas as her ideal model, fluent beyond her skill, then defers to Demosthenes, "that fluent sweet tongu'd Greek" who mended his natural incapacity by art. His example will not avail in her case; a lisp can be mended by art and "striving paine," but "A weak or wounded brain admits no cure." The poem then states the predicament of the woman poet, which is the emotional and rhetorical center of the piece:

> I am obnoxious to each carping tongue
> Who says my hand a needle better fits,
> A Poets pen all scorn I should thus wrong,
> For such despite they cast on Female wits:

If what I do prove well, it won't advance,
They'l say it's stoln, or else it was by chance.

(p. 119)

Stanza 6 begins her defense, summoning to her side the Nine Muses, in particular Calliope, mother of poetry, but she is careful to be doctrinally correct and call the Greeks foreigners who "play the fools and lye." Stanzas 7 and
8 bring the poem to a resigned close, acknowledging the superiority of men
and defining herself as the modest foil to the dazzling achievements of the
ruling sex:

7

Let Greeks be Greeks, and women what they are
Men have precedency and still excell,
It is but vain unjustly to wage warre;
Men can do best, and women know it well
Preheminence in all and each is yours;
Yet grant some small acknowledgement of ours.

8

And oh ye high flown quills that soar the Skies,
And ever with your prey still catch your praise,
If e'er you daigne these lowly lines your eyes
Give Thyme or Parsley wreath, I ask no bayes,
This mean and unrefined ure of mine
Will make your glistering gold but more to shine.

(p. 120)

A reading of Anne Bradstreet's other poems makes it clear that there is no
irony in these lines. She was the first known to us of the woman poets who
expressed in formal verse their plight as female poets, and her stanzas express
all the themes which characterize the *Apologia Pro Poemata Mea* as written by
female poets: the reluctant setting of limits to her poetic endeavors; the self-
justification against those who say she would do better to cultivate womanly
skills such as needlework; the anxiety lest, if what she write "prove well,"
"They'l say it's stoln"; the brief appeal to antique precedent; and the use of
diminishing[6]—and in this case domestic—images to refer to herself: "Give
Thyme or Parsley wreath, I ask no bayes."

Anne Killigrew's "Upon the Saying that my verses Were Made by Another"
is a bold and sometimes bitter poem, a record of her dedication, her rapture,

and her dismay and disappointment when her poems were declared to be written by another:

> Emboldened thus, to fame I did commit
> (By some few hands) my most unlucky wit.
> But ah, the sad effects that from it came!
> What ought t' have brought me honour, brought me shame!
> Like Aesop's painted jay, I seemed to all,
> Adorned in plumes, I not my own could call:
> Rifled like her, each one my feathers tore,
> And, as they thought, unto the owner bore.
> My laurels thus another's brow adorned,
> My numbers they admired, but me they scorned:
> Another's brow, that had so rich a store
> Of sacred wreaths that circled it before;
> While mine quite lost (like a small stream that ran
> Into a vast and boundless ocean,)
> Was swallowed up with what it joined, and drowned.
>
> (ll. 31–45)[7]

The movement of the poem is from aspiration to dejection to defiant determination. Her fate fulfills Anne Bradstreet's prophecy, "If what I do prove well . . . They'l say it's stoln." Like Anne Bradstreet, she describes herself as a poet in diminishing imagery—"like a small stream"—but her appeal is not with envy to a distant model; rather it is to a close and triumphant exemplar, Katherine Philips, the Matchless Orinda, and her invocation of classical precedent is not fugitive and hopeless but resolute, if ironic:

> The envious age, only to me alone,
> Will not allow what I do write, my own;
> But let them rage, and 'gainst a maid conspire,
> So deathless numbers from my tuneful lyre
> Do ever flow; so, Phoebus, I by thee
> Divinely inspired and possessed may be,
> I willingly accept Cassandra's fate,
> To speak the truth, although believed too late.
>
> (ll. 57–64)

Anne Finch's "The Introduction" is the best known of the poems in this vein. Though it begins with a complaint, "Alas," it is a high-spirited and determined piece, lacking the modest diffidence of Anne Bradstreet's poem and the sense of defiant outrage in Anne Killigrew's:

> Alas! a woman that attempts the pen,
> Such an intruder on the rights of men,
> Such a presumptuous Creature, is esteem'd,
> The fault, can by no vertue be redeem'd.
> They tell us, we mistake our sex and way;
> Good breeding, fassion, dancing, dressing, play
> Are the accomplishments we shou'd desire;
> To write, or read, or think, or to enquire
> Wou'd cloud our beauty, and exaust our time,
> And interrupt the Conquests of our prime;
> Whilst the dull mannage, of a servile house
> Is held by some, our outmost art, and use.
>
> (pp. 4–5, ll. 9–20)

Thus the poem begins with an elaboration of and implicitly a protest against received opinions about women. Anne Finch's appeal to antique precedent, which follows, is lengthy, substantial, and vigorous:

> Sure 'twas not ever thus, nor are we told
> Fables, of Women that excell'd of old;
> To whom, by the diffusive hand of Heaven
> Some share of witt, and poetry was given.
> . . . .
> A Woman here, leads fainting Israel on,
> She fights, she wins, she tryumphs with a song,
> Devout, Majestick, for the subject fitt,
> And far above her arms, exalts her witt,
> Then, to the peacefull, shady Palm withdraws,
> And rules the rescu'd Nation, with her Laws.
>
> (ll. 21–24, 45–50)

The poem moves to a resigned and diminished conclusion, somewhat like the general tone of Anne Bradstreet's poem:

> How are we fal'n, fal'n by mistaken rules?
> And Education's, more then Nature's fools,
> Debarr'd from all improve-ments of the mind,
> And to be dull, expected and dessigned;

And if some one, wou'd Soar above the rest,
With warmer fancy, and ambition press't,
So strong, th' opposing faction still appears,
The hopes to thrive, can ne're outweigh the fears,
Be caution'd then my Muse, and still retir'd;
Nor be dispis'd, aiming to be admir'd;
Conscious of wants, still with contracted wing,
To some few freinds, and to thy sorrows sing;
For groves of Lawrell, thou wert never meant;
Be dark enough thy shades, and be thou there content.

(ll. 51–64)

Unlike Anne Bradstreet, Anne Finch attributes the failure of women not to nature—"a weak or wounded brain"—but to faulty education. Yet she too, fearing the strength of "th' opposing faction," must content herself with a "contracted wing"—a small audience and a narrow range of song. Like Anne Bradstreet, who is content with a domestic herbal wreath of parsley or thyme, Anne Finch relinquished her aspirations to "groves of Lawrell."

The sense of plight shared by these more or less contemporaneous poems is clear, as is the common tone of constraint, defiance, and resourcefulness. From the formulation of the woman poet's predicament found in these poems, certain hypotheses about her work can be ventured. She will probably be uncertain in attempting major genres. She will experiment with some confidence in minor genres. She will cultivate modes which provide her with a persona or mask in the poem. She may use traditional fictions in a mocking manner which subverts their seriousness.[8] If the literary culture of her time provides a genre which allows her to express in poetry her sense of being an outsider, she will choose that genre. She may find in one particular traditional image a complex of associations which express her sense of herself in the tradition. A careful reading of Anne Finch's poems bears out these expectations.

The relation of literary theory to practice in the Restoration and early eighteenth century is problematical and variously interpreted. The fact that Anne Finch was a woman writer attempting to adapt her talents to a literary tradition from which women's voices were almost absent made her position as a writer in her time idiosyncratic. If Earl Miner is correct in seeing in the Restoration a shift from the private and coterie to the public mode,[9] and if critics of the period are right in their consensus that satire sets the dominant tone in the literature of the time, then Anne Finch's work is marginal to the literature of her age. She was not a satirist; in a prose statement she dissociated herself from satire's underhandedness and lack of charity. There is a satirical edge to her fables, epistles, and occasional poems; her life in retirement from the *beau monde* provided a distance across which she could view it with an ironic eye. But the themes of power, pretentiousness, and corruption in the public spheres of politics, established institutions, and high society, which provide the substance of much neoclassical satire, were not her concerns. When she turns her pen to the fates of kingdoms and monarchs, she expresses her sense of these affairs in older modes like the extended emblem. Satire is an aggressive mode, out for the kill or at least the exposé, and Anne Finch's sense of irony, which often included herself, undercuts the fiction of authority which satire requires.

Thus temperament, and the voice which expresses temperament, influence a poet's choice of genre, which Frank Kermode calls the first of the "constraints which shadow interpretation."[10] And for a woman poet in the late seventeenth century there was a condition prior to the constraints of genre: the constraint of being a woman. The fact that Anne Finch turns repeatedly in poems to her concern with her vocation as a poet who is also a woman suggests that it constitutes an essential knot which she by turns entwines, embellishes, or attempts to untie. The combination woman/poet presents at various times a paradox, a mystery, a scandal, an oxymoron, and a triumph. This concern haunts her poetry, sometimes on the periphery, as a distraction or obstacle which must be dealt with before she can get to her theme, sometimes, as in "The Appology," as her subject itself. In these ironic lines she disarms anxiously anticipated criticism by belittling her accomplishments as a poet and at the same time using received opinion about women—"Each Woman has her weaknesse"—to argue her case for her persistence in writing poetry:

> 'Tis true I write and tell me by what Rule
> I am alone forbid to play the fool
> To follow through the Groves a wand'ring Muse
> And fain'd Idea's for my pleasures chuse
> Why shou'd it in my Pen be held a fault
> Whilst Mira paints her face, to paint a thought
> Whilst Lamia to the manly Bumper flys
> And borrow'd Spiritts sparkle in her Eyes
> Why shou'd itt be in me a thing so vain
> To heat with Poetry my colder Brain. . . .
> (p. 13, ll. 1–10)

The paired comparisons which express her ironic deprecation of her choice of folly point to the higher value of her unfeminine predilections, but the use of rhetorical questions rather than assertions suggests that her weakness is not likely to be viewed with sympathy by those to whom the poem is addressed.

There is a telling passage about her poetic aspirations enclosed in the formal epistle, "To the Honorable the Lady Worsley at Longleate," an extended compliment to a style of life and writing and a concentrated topographical poem in the vein of Marvell's "Upon Appleton House":

> Cou'd but the Witt that on her paper flows
> Affect my Verse and tune itt to her Prose
> Through every Line a kindly warmth inspire
> And raise my Art equal to my desire
> Then shou'd my Hand snatch from the Muses store
> Transporting Figures n'ere expos'd before
> Somthing to Please so moving and so new
> As not our Denham or our Cowley knew.
>
> (p. 53, ll. 37–44)

The "Cou'd but . . . Then" construction in this passage points to the tension in her poetry between ambition and accomplishment, but her longing to outdo the esteemed Denham and Cowley suggests the scope of her ambition.

"An Epistle From Ardelia to Mrs. Randolph in answer to her Poem upon Her Verses" gives Anne Finch the occasion to claim for her sex their ancient rights to poetry—not in her own name, for her defensive mask of modesty forbids her to do so, but in the name of a sister poet:

> Madam,
>   till pow'rfully convinc'd by you,
> I thought those Praises never were Their due,
> Which I had read, or heard bestow'd by Men
> On Women, that have ventur'd on the Pen.
> But now must yeild (pursuaded by your stile)
> That Lesbian Sapho's might all hearts beguile.
> The vanquish'd Pindar, now I must beleive
> Might from Corrina's Muse new Laws receive,
> Since our own Age is happily possest
> Of such a genius, in a Female Breast,
> As gives us Faith for all those wonders told,
> Producing New, to justify the old.
> Then we'll no more submitt, but (in your name)
> To Poetry renew our Ancient Claime;
> Through itts retirement, we'll your worth persue
> And lead itt into Public Rule and view. . . .
>
> (p. 95, ll. 1–16)

The formal complexity of these lines shows Anne Finch's mastery of the subtleties of neoclassical style. This brief poem is a compliment enclosed in an epistle which also encompasses a panegyric to friendship and—in the lines quoted—a manifesto of women's ancient rights to poetry.

The lovely, varied lyric, "Melinda on an Insippid Beauty In imitation of a fragment of Sapho's," combines the old *memento mori* theme with the equally old conceit concerning the poet's fame after death to make a poem which is the boldest statement Anne Finch ever ventured about the worth of her poetic endeavors. It accords with what we know of her temperament that she could make such a strong assertion only through the persona of Sappho, acknowledged paradigm of women poets:

> You, when your body, life shall leave
> Must drop entire, into the grave;
> Unheeded, unregarded lye,
> And all of you together dye;
> Must hide that fleeting charm, that face in dust,
> Or to some painted cloath, the slighted Immage trust,
> Whilst my fam'd works, shall throo' all times surprise
> My polish'd thoughts, my bright Ideas rise,
> And to new men be known, still talking to their eyes.
>
> (p. 122, ll. 1–9)

This brief poem has great formal beauty. It imitates in its changing line length the movement of its thought from the confinement of death to the freedom of living in spirit after death, through poetry. The poet, as she often does, balances the poem on a contrast between the conventional image of the feminine and her own sense of poetic vocation, but this lyric is free from defensiveness. It states with clear authority, without question, condition, or qualification, her expectation of poetic renown. It is characteristic of her ironic wit that she envisions her triumph, immortality through her poems, in terms of feminine conquest—"And to new men be known, still talking to their eyes."

In spite of such affirmations as the one expressed in this poem, it remains true that Anne Finch's poetic vocation marked her, in her time, as eccentric. As the poems earlier quoted by Anne Bradstreet, Anne Killigrew, and Anne Finch show, literature was still considered the province of men, and women ventured into their territory with trepidation and at the risk of scorn. Anne Finch availed herself of various stratagems for surviving as an eccentric—a versifying lady. One device, as in the lyric just quoted, was to speak through the voice of a recognized and lauded paradigm like Sappho. Another was to make common cause with fellow eccentrics. This she does humorously in the "The Circuit of

Appollo," a whimsical description of a contest among women poets, probably modeled on Suckling's "A Session of the Poets," and seriously in such poems as the epistle to Mrs. Randolph discussed above and in her lines "To a Fellow Scribbler," an intricate extended emblem. Written in a poetic convention which links its author with early seventeenth-century poets, it expresses forcefully Anne Finch's anxiety lest, after all, "we rhiming fools" may have spent life in "vain flourish":

> Unless we solidly indite,
> Some good infusing while we write,
>
> . . . .
>
> We like that tree and hedge be found,
> Grotesque and trivial, shun'd by all,
> And soon forgotten when we fall.
> (p. 106, ll. 28–9, 31–33)

Her misgivings about the worthwhileness of "scribbling" are common to all authors on occasion, but there is a shudder in the words "Grotesque and trivial, shun'd by all," which can be linked to her apprehension, expressed in other poems, that her deviance in being a woman writer will cause her to be despised and condemned by the world.

Another tactic is to describe oneself as deviant in a way which allows such eccentricities as the writing of poetry. By presenting herself in a number of poems as melancholy, a prisoner of Spleen, Anne Finch provided an image of herself which gave a certain licence to her odd persistence in following her Muse. That she did indeed suffer from this malady is documented by Reynolds (pp. lxii–lxiv). In her poems, her fits of depression are linked in various ways to her writing of poetry. In "Ardelia to Melancholy" she invokes poetry as an attempted cure for the "dusky, sullen foe" which acts the Tyrant in her "darken'd breast" (p. 15). In "The Spleen" her malady is described as inimical to her poetic powers:

> O'er me alas! thou dost too much prevail:
> I feel thy Force, whilst I against thee rail;
> I feel my Verse decay, and my crampt Numbers fail.
> Thro' thy black Jaundice I all Objects see,
>   As Dark, and Terrible as Thee,
> My Lines decry'd, and my Employment thought
> An useless Folly, or presumptuous Fault.
> (p. 250, ll. 74–80)

43

"The Spleen" is a Pindaric ode composed in neoclassical style, to which this set piece of confession is incidental. But these lines do suggest that her moods of melancholy undermine her confidence in her "Employment," her poetic vocation. The notions of "Folly" and "Fault" are elaborated in the justly famous passage in which she declares her choice of eccentricity and eloquently justifies it in comparison with the accomplishments which social conventions encourage in women:

> Whilst in the *Muses* Paths I stray,
> Whilst in their Groves, and by their secret Springs
> My Hand delights to trace unusual Things,
> And deviates from the known, and common way;
>   Nor will in fading Silks compose
>   Faintly th' inimitable *Rose*,
> Fill up an ill-drawn *Bird*, or paint on Glass
> The *Sov'reign's* blurr'd and undistinguish'd Face,
> The threatning *Angel*, and the speaking *Ass*.
>
>   (p. 250, ll. 81–89)

This lovely passage presents an image in miniature of Anne Finch's achievements as a poet. It expresses in fine epitome her own sense of her dubious rarity, her resolute refusal of conventional womanly accomplishments, the whole couched in a style which displays her mastery of the refinements of neoclassical poetic convention, especially in her choice of epithets and her striking nouns which capture both the image and the type.

The source of the strength which enabled her to make such a daring refusal was her clear sense of vocation. Underneath the apologies, justifications, brooding inquiries, and rueful jests lies her unquenchable delight in writing. She tried to give it up, but by her own account she found herself to be "like those imperfect penitents, who are ever relenting, and yett ever returning to the same offences . . . till at last (like them) wearied with uncertainty, and irresolution, I rather chuse to be harden'd in an errour, then to be still att the trouble of endeavering to over come itt: and now, neither deny myself the pleasure of writing, or any longer make a mistery to that of my freinds and acquaintance, which does so little deserve itt" (p. 7). The personal narrative of conflict and self-doubt suggested by this passage can only be inferred from her words. What is clear is that some of her best poetry arises out of the very conflict between aspiration and denial, between poetic vocation and social convention, which is expressed with such restraint in this prose passage.

44

Up to a point, constraints challenge invention, so long as the constraints do not amount to an interdiction. Certain formal constraints provide opportunities. In making poetry out of her predicament of being both woman and poet, Anne Finch joined the honorable tradition of poets, both men and women, who have turned their plights to poetry. Out of the constraints of being a gentlewoman, Anne Finch wrote many occasional poems elaborating the courtesies of friendship, hospitality, marriage, mourning, anniversaries, and the like, weaving through poems the network of observance and exchange which women were then, as they are now, expected to sustain. Some of these pieces we find delightful still, some seem tenuous and faded at this distance from the social occasions which evoked them, but all of them provided her with an opportunity to compose poetry. Occasional poetry was still considered a literary convention of some merit, and it was natural for her to turn to poetry to express socially and religiously sanctioned feelings. Besides formal poems written for weddings and funerals, and poems paying respects to mentors and betters, her occasional poems are most often devoted to personal friendship, a theme which occupies an important place in her "Petition for an Absolute Retreat." The pastoral fiction involving Arcadian names links her occasional poems to her more personal verse epistles and love poems to her husband. Her sense of personal and social obligation was strong, and it is touching to see her turning her poetic talents to the woman's work of attending to the courtesies of life's great and small occasions. The poetic decorum governing such pieces still in her time provided a readily available set of conventions, and her position as a gentlewoman must have made very vivid to her her sense of obligation in the matter of observing occasions.

Not that she would have thought being a gentlewoman a constraint, chafe as she did against the triviality of the slight accomplishments expected of women of refinement. Like her religious faith, being a gentlewoman was the condition to which God's providence had called her. The one constraint which riled her was that her calling to write poetry was at odds with the other callings. The predicament of being both female and a poet creates a kind of ground base or undersong to all of Anne Finch's work. Both a plight and a challenge, it is like a given tone or key signature which governs the melodies she elaborates.[11]

The condition of being formed "of Female clay," fashioned as one of the "weaker kinde," is not in itself a circumstance she chafes at. Poems like "Fragment," a kind of progress of the soul, and "On Myselfe," start with women's inferior nature as a given. What is intolerable to her is that a codicil to the decree of female inferiority should be that women are not allowed to write poetry. Her outrage at the injustice of this prohibition is interestingly transferred from the art of poetry to the art of tapestry weaving, in "A Description of One of the Pieces of Tapistry at Long-Leat" (p. 47). In the introductory stanza she establishes the honorable tradition of tapestry weaving by women, which allowed them to share in the toil and the fame of their illustrious husbands' heroic deeds. A brief complaint provides a transition to the rhetoric of her own struggle to seize her subject with confidence:

> No longer, *Females* to such Praise aspire,
> And seldom now We rightly do admire.
> So much, All Arts are by the *Men* engross'd,
> And Our few Talents unimprov'd or cross'd. . . .
>
> (ll. 10–13)

The lines following this description of the general plight of women in relation to knowledge of or skill in practicing the arts include herself in their shared deprivation. The rhetoric of modesty in the face of the task of describing renowned works of art is part of the convention of the self-deprecating preamble, but the wistful evocation of the antique days when women were preeminent as weavers and the rueful protest against the trespassing of men mark this passage as another instance in which the poet cries out against the obstacles placed in her path as a poet who is a woman:

> Even I, who on this Subject wou'd compose,
> Which the fam'd *Urbin* for his Pencil chose,
>
> . . . .
>
> Shou'd prudently from the Attempt withdraw,
> But Inclination proves the stronger Law:
> And tho' the Censures of the World pursue
> These hardy Flights, whilst his *Designs* I view;
> My burden'd Thoughts, which labour for a Vent,
> Urge me t' explain in Verse, what by each Face is meant.
>
> (ll. 14–15, 18–23)

This movement from aspiration to discouragement to resolve is repeated over and over in Anne Finch's poetry. The mixed apprehension and boldness which she feels as a woman who dares to follow her muse and write energizes some of her most vivid poems. Had she not felt her plight so sensitively she would not interest us as she now does. She springs to life as we watch her, in the lines of her poetry, first pinioned by self-doubt and fear of disparagement, then breaking free and getting on with her poem.

In approaching Anne Finch's choice of form and subject within the frame of her predicament as a woman poet, we are fortunate in having a poem in which she writes about poetic genres. "The Critick and the Writer of Fables" talks about her choice of fable as a vehicle for expressing her vivid sense of life and manners, and briefly gives her views about some of the other genres—Pindaric, pastoral, heroic, and satiric. Since the subject of the poem is her preference for fable, her description of the other genres is diminishing, but her remarks about the kinds which she is rhetorically rejecting are nonetheless illuminating. She does not mention the occasional poem or the varied lyric, both kinds to which she devoted a good deal of her poetic energy. She may have considered these minor kinds to be so familiar in both the literary and the ordinary sense that their characteristics did not need comment.

The poem begins with a narrative about her surfeit of Pindarics, described correctly according to the canons of her day as an adventuresome, wandering mode:

> Weary, at last, of the *Pindarick* way,
> Thro' which advent'rously the Muse wou'd stray;
> To *Fable* I descend with the soft Delight,
> Pleas'd to Translate, or easily Endite:
> Whilst aery Fictions hastily repair
> To fill my Page, and rid my thoughts of Care,
> As they to Birds and Beasts new Gifts impart,
> And Teach, as Poets shou'd, whilst they Divert.
>
> (p. 153, ll. 1–8)

She must "descend" to the fable because it was thought of as a base or mean genre. The lowly fable has, for her, the virtue of distracting her from care with its "aery Fictions" which yet fulfill the traditional task of the poet—to teach and to delight. The argument develops as a dialogue between a critic, who disdains the writer of fables as a lazy trifler, and the poet, who dismisses the alternatives offered by the critic. She justifies her preference by exaggerating the excesses of the other genres: the pedantic bombast of heroic; the insipid, faded, amorous cliché of pastoral's counterfeit dream; the spiteful malice which guides the satirist's pen.

Though "The Critick and the Writer of Fables" is an occasional piece written as a preface to her own fables, its remarks about genre are illuminating in light of Anne Finch's choice of genres. The heroic vein rejected in the poem she never essayed, not even in that short-lived subgenre, the heroic drama: both her closet plays look back to earlier modes, one being a tragicomedy, the other a tragedy. In preferring the mock-heroic which, as we shall see, she uses in some of her fables, in "The Spleen," and in certain occasional poems, she is typical of her time. Pastoral, the next mode which the poem rejects, had its uses for her. Adapting one of its conventions, she created for herself a bucolic poetic persona, Ardelia, who could embody and express at one remove a whole complex of values and feelings. In one long poem, "Upon the Death of Sir William Twisden," she uses pastoral convention in a serious exercise in the elegiac mode. But even here, as Reynolds has observed (pp. cxxx–cxxxi), she undermines the pastoral convention that nature mourns the death of the departed by calling it a poetic dream. The fictions of the pastoral elegy can no longer for her embody the anguish of deep grief. In her rejection of pastoral for profound occasions she is at one with her time. By the late seventeenth century pastoral conventions were no longer used for high serious poetry.

One convention from pastoral romance did provide her with a fiction in terms of which she could tenderly and sometimes playfully elaborate the love between herself and her husband under the guise of Ardelia and Dafnis, or Flavio. Two of the poems she composed using this pastoral code express her oblique relationship as a poet to the traditions of love poetry. They show us a woman poet adapting herself to the tradition as she knows it, picking her literary models against the fashion of her time, in order to be true to her subject. In Restoration poetry the dominant strain in love poetry was illicit and often licentious. Anne Finch's love poems, in contrast, reach back to the earlier tradition of the sonnets of Spenser and Sidney which praise fidelity in love.[12] Her affinity for this "fashion past" in courtship and poetry is made explicit in another poem, "The Prodigy," which begins in a tone of mocking hyperbole and develops into a poem of instruction to the fair sex, in the course of which she invokes the authority of the older poets:

> How chang'd is Britain to the blooming fair,
> Whom now the men no longer make their care;
>
> . . . .
>
> Not so (as still declare their works) it prov'd
> When Spencer, Sydney, and when Waller lov'd,
> Who with soft numbers wing'd successful darts. . . .
> (p. 143, ll. 13–14, 17–19)

The first of the two poems to her husband, "To Mr. F. Now Earl of W.," moves through a lively narrative about the poet's search for inspiration to a conclusion which restates the commonplace enshrined in Sidney's "Fool, said my Muse to me, look in thy heart, and write!" The subject of the poem is at one level her love for her husband, at another the difficulty of invention when your theme is not countenanced by the fashions governing the genre in which you are writing. Ardelia's posture throughout the poem is that of the obedient wife of a husband "who indulg'd her Verse, / And now requir'd her Rimes"

(p. 21, ll. 35–36). Eager to oblige him with a poem on his return, she sends to Parnassus to beg assistance of the Muses in writing a poem in his praise. Her unusual request causes consternation:

> A *Husband*! eccho'd all around:
> And to *Parnassus* sure that Sound
>   Had never yet been sent;
> Amazement in each Face was read,
> In haste th' affrighted Sisters fled,
>   And unto Council went.
>   (ll. 37–42)

It seems that her subject is a matter for old ballads and romances. The Muses cannot provide a scheme of invention for such an outmoded design. None of them will touch it except for Urania, who advises her to "dictate from the Heart." Ardelia,

> Consulting now her Breast,
> Perceiv'd that ev'ry tender Thought,
> Which from abroad she'd vainly sought,
>   Did there in Silence rest. . . .
>   (p. 23, ll. 81–84)

The poem concludes with an inspired comment on the poem's larger subject— her fortunate eccentricity in being the unfashionable poet of married love:

> For since the World do's so despise
> *Hymen's* Endearments and its Ties,
>   They shou'd mysterious be;
> Till We that Pleasure too possess
> (Which makes their fancy'd Happiness)
>   Of stollen Secrecy.
>   (ll. 91–96)

The notion that true love is and ought to be a hidden mystery, unutterable except between lover and beloved, reached its utmost expression in English poetry in Donne's love poems, and in this final stanza which expresses her disinclination to tell the laity her love, Anne Finch places herself in that refined tradition.

The second poem, "An Invitation to Dafnis," adapts the conventions of the seduction poem so popular with Cavalier and Restoration poets, with its refrain based on the alluring "Come . . . ," to an invitation to her husband to leave his indoor pursuits and "throo' the groves, with your Ardelia stray"(p. 28). This piece plays upon the very old contrast between art and nature, and it reconciles the *carpe diem* motif, which in Cavalier poetry had erotic associations, with the innocent mutual enjoyment of the pleasures of the countryside. The substance of the poem is the contrast between the sedentary and learned pursuits which she beseeches Dafnis to abandon and the "rural joys" of "plainer Nature." As an invitation poem there is nothing like it until Wordsworth's "The Tables Turned" with its call, "Up! up! my friend, and quit your books." But "An Invitation" is an occasional poem contrasting indoor and outdoor pleasures and stressing shared happiness in nature. Wordsworth's poem, though it too turns on the contrast between Nature on the one hand and Science and Art on the other, turns the contrast into the doctrine that Nature is the best teacher of the nature of man and of moral good and evil—advice which Anne Finch would find incomprehensible. Still, to echo and rectify Herrick and to anticipate Wordsworth in one poem is no mean accomplishment. That Anne Finch encompassed in one occasional poem both the Cavalier poet in his itemization of rural delights and the Romantic poet in his inspired morality shows her inventiveness in adapting the main tradition to her own purposes as devoted wife and poet.

In such poems as "A Pastoral Dialogue" and "The Cautious Lovers," she devises a slender pastoral fiction in order to comment on the vagaries of love. In a wide range of poems of address to friends both male and female, she uses names from pastoral tradition: Ephelia, Arminda, Serena. This practice was common in the writing of polite occasional verse. It allowed her as a lady to express feeling without violating the social decorum governing her class and sex or the literary decorum which in the main allowed the expression of emotion only within the frame of fiction.

She also wrote an ambitious pastoral poem "Between Menalcus and Damon, on the Appearance of the Angels to the Shepheards on Our Saviour's Birth Day." This blending of the pastoral imagery from classical and Christian sources was sanctioned by a long tradition, but it seems to require a poet like Milton, whose imagination was deeply engaged with both sources, to fuse into poetry. Anne Finch's piece has some lovely detail, its couplets are varied with a refrain in Alexandrines, and it contains traces of her reading of Milton, but she does not manage to blend the diction of pastoral with the vocabulary of the Bible, and the flaw of over-ornamentation which dogs her heels when she is uninspired drags the poem down.

Satire, the third mode rejected in "The Critick and the Writer of Fables," was the dominant mode of her day. Of it she says in her prose statement "The Preface":

As to Lampoons, and all sorts of abusive verses, I ever so much detested, both the underhand dealing and uncharitablenesse which accompanys them, that I never suffer'd my small talent, to be that way employ'd. . . . The only coppy of mine that tends toward this, is the letter to Ephelia, in answer to an invitation to the Town; . . . so I do declare, that att the time of composing itt, there was no particular person meant by any of the disadvantageous Caracters; and the whole intention of itt, was in general to expose the Censorious humour, foppishnesse and coquetterie that then prevail'd. And I am so far from thinking there is any ill in this, that I wish itt oftener done, by such hands as might sufficiently ridicule, and wean us from those mistakes in our manners, and conversation.

(pp. 10–11)

The poem referred to, "Ardelia's Answer to Ephelia," is a sprightly essay in the Horatian manner. Framed like Donne's Satire IV by a visit from country to town, the poem displays a series of satiric set pieces of contemporary types and manners: the wit, the fop, the faded beauty. Among them a woman writer is displayed:

> Now what's that thing, she crys, Ardelia, guesse?
> A woman sure.—
>   Ay and a Poetesse,
> They say she writes, and 'tis a comon jest.
>   (p. 44, ll. 194–97)

Ardelia replies by listing the reasons for which the poetess must be the object of scorn. She must surely have professed her skill publicly, shown pride in her gift, written spiteful satires more full of spleen than wit, published under her own name a song which exposes her to all social ranks, or had lines of her poetry inscribed on an allegorical picture of herself crowned with laurel. If a woman writer commits none of these affronts, Ardelia asks,

> Why shou'd we from that pleasing art be ty'd,
> Or like State Pris'ners, Pen and Ink deny'd?
>   (ll. 208–9)

What is revealed in this passage is Anne Finch's view of how circumspect a woman poet must be to escape censure and continue to write with impunity.

In keeping with Anne Finch's misgivings about abusive satire, as expressed in the prose passage just quoted, Almeria, who speaks most of the splenetic, harsh lines, is herself displayed as indolent, vain and shallow, while Ardelia, the persona of the poet, is presented as a naive, trusting, openhearted countrywoman. Almeria's voice is shallowly cynical rather than satirical, and the two points of view together make a double focus, a complex perspective which deepens the moral tone of the poem. The whole piece is sustained by the dauntless good hope of Ardelia and the arch worldliness of the supercilious Almeria. Through Ardelia's bewilderment at the gaudy and grotesque Vanity Fair of the town, the poem conveys the pathos of lives so superficially led. The object of the satire is double: the counterfeit world of high life, and those like Almeria who compound by a kind of moral double-dealing their involvement in a depraved milieu of which they pretend to be weary but which they cannot relinquish.

Anne Finch did not essay many sustained satires, though there are satiric touches in a number of her poems and her "Adam Pos'd" is, as Ann Messenger has described it, a "brief, almost epigrammatic Augustan satire dealing with moral implications, for all its brevity, nearly as wide-ranging as Donne's."[13] Invective and vehement satire were alien to her sensibility and she had a firm sense of propriety about the diction allowable to a lady. The satiric passages in her poems are most often sallies in an ironic tone, ranging from the playful to the sardonic. The objects of her satire are usually affectation and the folly of what the world calls love. Her fables, which treat specific instances of human foolishness displayed in exemplary tales, comment satirically on a wide range of human frailties, from our addle-headedness in taking advice, through our overweening fondness for giving it, our propensity to think others better off than we are, our inflated fondness for our own kind and kin, and the frequent and often ludicrous failure of our protective stratagems.

"An Epilogue to the Tragedy of Jane Shore" is obliquely satirical in its wry comment on the different criteria by which men and women are valued in the world. A bold and high-spirited occasional piece, written to be spoken in public by the actress playing the part of Jane Shore, it works through ironies created by the distances between the three personae invoked: the poet; the actress, Mrs. Oldfield; and Jane Shore. The elegiac note in the satirical lines on the double standard for judging men and women is characteristic of the subtlety of Anne Finch's style.

> There is a season, which too fast approaches,
> And every list'ning beauty nearly touches;
> When handsome Ladies, falling to decay,
> Pass thro' new epithets to smooth the way:
> From *fair* and *young* transportedly confess'd,
> Dwindle to *fine, well fashion'd,* and *well dress'd.*
> Thence as their fortitude's extremest proof,
> To *well as yet;* from *well* to *well enough;*

Till having on such weak foundation stood,
Deplorably at last they sink to *good.*
Abandon'd then, 'tis time to be retir'd,
And seen no more, when not alas! admir'd.
By men indeed a better fate is known.
The pretty fellow, that has youth outgrown,
Who nothing knew, but how his cloaths did sit,
Transforms to a *Free-thinker* and a *Wit;*
At Operas becomes a skill'd Musician;
Ends in a partyman and politician;
Maintains some figure, while he keeps his breath,
And is a fop of consequence till death.

(p. 101, ll. 27–46)

There is a satiric edge to the lyric "The Unequal Fetters," a witty, disillusioned rejection of marriage based, like the "Epilogue," on the inequality between men and women:

Free as Nature's first intention
   Was to make us, I'll be found
Nor by subtle Man's invention
   Yeild to be in Fetters bound
By one that walks a freer round.

Mariage does but slightly tye Men
   Whil'st close Pris'ners we remain
They the larger Slaves of Hymen
   Still are begging Love again
At the full length of all their chain.

(p. 151, ll. 11–20)

This dispraise of the married state as it concerns women is not to be taken as the poet's own opinion, since we know from her own testimony that her marriage was happy. But it shows her skill in the concentrated ironic lyric. The *double entendre* in the last stanza, suggesting that while men have more freedom in marriage they are still the slaves of love, is typical of the subtle double focus of her satire.

But her response in "The Critick and the Writer of Fables" to the critic's exhortations to write satire suggest that she was not by nature and inclination a satirist. "Then," she enquires in the persona of the poet, "must that single Stream the Town supply, / . . . And all the Rest of *Helicon* be dry?" (p. 155).

It was otherwise with the Pindaric. Though—if the narrative of her choice of genres in "The Critick" can be taken as something other than an apology for turning the "harmless *Fable*-writer"—she eventually wearied of "the *Pindarick* way," she was initially drawn to it and what is probably her best-known poem, "The Spleen," is a Pindaric ode.

The form of the Pindaric was, according to Ruth Wallerstein, established by Cowley as the standard form for high occasional poetry. It was characterized by embellishment, amplification, an "enthusiastic attack upon great concepts and intellectual events," a "bold play of figures and ideas," and a "large and varied metrical structure."[14]

Cowley was important to Anne Finch as a model in two ways: as "the great exponent of the *beatus ille* theme,"[15] the tradition to which her poems of retirement belong, and as the model for the Pindaric ode which, in his hands, developed a loose, variable structure, and emphasized enthusiasm moving toward rapture, rather than rational argument.[16] Reynolds says of Anne Finch's Pindarics:

> But the school of Cowley held that the true pindaric marks were exalted themes, striking and unusual figures, abrupt transitions, impetuosity and excitement of mood, with an extreme complexity and irregularity of stanzaic structure and rhyme scheme. Lady Winchilsea's three *Odes* come between 1694 and 1703, hence they belong to the last period of Cowley's influence and just before the reactionary period set in. She called Cowley master, and theoretically she accepted his pindaric conventions; but her *Odes,* while irregular, are not markedly so, nor have they any of the "flights" of Cowley's *Odes,* nor any of the conceits.

> (p. cvii)

By the time Johnson wrote his life of Cowley, the Pindaric was viewed as an invitation to write nonsense garbed in immoderate language, but during the Restoration and the early eighteenth century it was still a respected form. The Pindaric allowed digression and amplification. Anne Finch says that her Muse strayed adventurously in the Pindaric way. "Way" suggests direction and purpose, adventurous straying suggests the welcome opportunity to allow the attention to be captured by and the feet to follow after bright attractive things slightly off the beaten track of the poem. We know from the confessional passage in "The Spleen" that she liked "to deviate from the known, and common way"; the Pindaric may have appealed to this quality in her. The form was admired and practiced by Cowley, with whom she shared Royalist political sympathies and to whom she looked as a mentor for her poems of retirement. We know that she did not feel at ease in satire, the dominant mode of her time, and the Pindaric ode provided an opportunity to treat serious themes on an ambitious scale.

"All is Vanity," the least remarkable of her odes, begins with an elaboration of the *sic vita* theme, rather in the Elizabethan manner, with images drawn from the transient in nature—plants, clouds, leaves, bubbles, dreams. It moves through the expected paradigms of human aspiration and defeat, exempla illustrating the vanity of human wishes. While relying on commonplaces in passages remote from her sensibility, she is inventive in vignettes which arouse her sympathy, like the spectacle of Antony succumbing to the charms of Cleopatra.

> On a resplendent and conspicuous Bed,
> With all the Pride of *Persia* loosely spread,
>   The lovely *Syrene* lay.
> Which but discern'd from the yet distant Shore,
> Th' amazed Emperor could hate no more;
> No more a baffled Vengeance could pursue;
> But yielding still, still as she nearer drew,
> When *Cleopatra* anchor'd in the Bay,
> Where every Charm cou'd all its Force display,
> Like his own *Statue* stood, and gaz'd the *World* away.
>   (p. 243, ll. 145–54)

She warms, too, to her description of the inflated ambition of the poet who aspires to eternal renown. Had not she herself in "Melinda on an Insippid Beauty" envisaged the triumph of poetic fame? In a similar vein the poet in "All is Vanity" vaunts that "when his Body falls in Funeral Fire / . . . His name shall live, and his best Part aspire." The conventions of the poem require that the "Deluded Wretch" be chastised for his overweening ambition, but her lively depiction of his imagined renown and her severe deflation of the hyperbole of his "enchanted Palace in the Air" suggest her sympathy with his particular vanity. Anne Finch was a poet with high moral standards, and this poem allows her to have her cake and eat it, to depict the pleasures of the world with delight and then to condemn what she has feelingly described.

The Pindaric allowed strong passages in which her enthusiasms could soar, but one of the hazards of the form, which calls for an elevated conception of its subject and a consistently high style, is that "such a style may go wrong in trying to deal with familiar or commonplace events for which a demotic style would be more appropriate."[17] In Anne Finch's Pindaric ode "Upon the Hurricane in November 1703," the continuous elevation of tone required by the serious Pindaric and the lofty diction that the tone demands are often at odds with the material. Hence the poem is an act of literary virtuosity which does not work. Adventuresome, dazzling in scope, intermittently brilliant, it is nonetheless flawed, because the constraints of the form do not accord with the subject.

"The Spleen, A Pindarick Poem" is, in contrast, unfalteringly successful, and it is interesting to consider why. This poem is related to high Pindaric as mock-heroic is related to serious heroic. The form is sustained and exploited with ingenuity, but the subject is treated with an irony which, while not precluding seriousness, maintains a tone of playful mockery. The contrast between form and tone creates an aesthetic distance similar to that which Pope explores at greater length and with subtle effect in *The Rape of the Lock*. The subject is by turns elevated and diminished, and the gravity of those splenetic unfortunates who take themselves and their condition seriously—including the author of a poem which purports to take the spleen with high seriousness—is archly mocked. The controlling tone of the poem is a civility which never deserts Anne Finch, even in her melancholy moods, which modulates her satire and takes the edge off her severe morality. Her voice in "The Spleen" ranges through the urbane, the playful, to a kind of scornful *hauteur,* but it is always the modulated voice of a lady. It could not be otherwise. The poem is contrived to give expression to her various talents: her high spirits, her gift for descriptive vignettes, her flair for light social satire, and her confessional vein. The poem anatomizes Spleen, animates it, gives it a myth of origin going back to the Fall, and displays it in its various Protean disguises. The well-known confessional piece in the center of the poem, quoted earlier, is not an intrusion on the form but a decorous instance in her anatomy of the malady. The poignant glimpse given in this passage of the despair which overwhelmed her when she lost faith in her poetic vocation is made doubly moving by its appearance in a poem of elegant, controlled artifice. In this high-spirited *jeu d'esprit,* at once a complaint and a reluctant tribute, Anne Finch shows herself to be mistress of her malady by fettering it in verse.

The Pindaric had been a major mode but it was going out of style; the fable was a minor mode but it was new and it provided her with an ideal medium for her gift for bright particulars and conversational English, and her interest in moral improvement. It allowed her to indulge her pleasure in the racy and the picturesque because the embellishments in the fable were provided in the service of a moral lesson. In deciding to versify fables, she shrewdly chose a mode which gave her varied talents scope.

Donald Davie, writing about Gay as a fabulist, says that the writer of fables is "a moralist peculiarly interested in the animal creation as a hierarchy of signs acknowledging the creative wisdom."[18] Anne Finch had something no less serious but somewhat less elevated in mind. Most often it is worldly wisdom rather than the Creator's wisdom that her fables wryly point out. In her lines "To Mr. Pope," she cautioned him that his tales should be "easy, natural, and gay"—gentle counsel, as she calls it, which she herself followed. Her fables are conversational and lively, her narrative style brisk. She uses embellishment decorously, either graphically as the situation calls for it, or ironically as the moral requires it. She always remembers that she is telling a story which must at every point engage and hold the attention of the listener.

There are some thirty-five fables in her published poems, in a variety of meters, all of them lively, energetic, and readable. For a poet whose weakness is for inappropriate embellishment, the fable offered a discipline which clarified her style. In a fable the narrative line is given; invention is concerned not with substance but with detail, which must be pertinent because fables are always on the brief side, like embellished exempla. The tightness of the story to be told kept her gift for ornament in line. Like all good stories, her fables begin briskly with a noun and a verb and continue with a strong sense of direction to their necessary end: a conclusion and a moral. This final application or caution-ary ending invited pointed but oblique commentary on human nature. This stance suited Anne Finch's temperament, her life at one remove from the busy world, and her gender, which made authoritative moral pronouncements out of the question.

Anne Finch was something of an innovator in her fables, as Myra Reynolds makes convincingly clear:

> At the beginning of the eighteenth century there was a new and wide-spread interest in fables. English prose versions of *Aesop* had held their place in popular favor from the days of Caxton down, and the Latin *Aesop* was in use in the schools, but it is to La Fontaine that this striking revival of interest is chiefly due. The first six books of his *Fables* were published in France in 1668, other parts appearing in 1671, 1678, 1679, and the twelve books in 1694. Their popularity in England is shown by a remark of Addison, who, writing in 1711 in praise of fables, says that La Fontaine "by this way of writing is come into vogue more than any other Author of our times." . . . Gay has always been counted the progenitor of the race of verse fable-writers in England. . . . [But] the fact stands that before Gay, Lady Winchilsea holds a solitary pre-eminence as an English fable-writer in the manner of La Fontaine. . . . She formed herself almost entirely on La Fontaine, who had broken distinctly with the literary traditions of his predecessors. It had been said that the ornament of the fable was no ornament, that brevity and conciseness were essential, that morals must be explicitly stated. But La Fontaine deliberately challenged this concep-tion. He set himself . . . to add to them something of novelty and adorn-ment. . . . It was to this fable convention that Lady Winchilsea gave allegiance.

> (pp. cviii–cix)

Anne Finch, Reynolds goes on, did not attempt originality of invention, but relied on models which she followed with the degree of fidelity which suited her intention. In general she treats her material with great freedom, inventing details, altering her "morals," but holding throughout to La Fontaine's ideal of smooth, graceful, amplified narration.

Her civility, her diffidence, her playful sense of humor, her viewing the vagaries of the world from some distance—all these qualities would make attractive to her the urbane, unassertive, light touch of La Fontaine. One fable which shows how adroitly she adopted her model to suit her own voice and circumstances is "The Goute and Spider: A Fable Imitated from Monsr. de la Fontaine And Inscribed to Mr. Finch After his first Fitt of that Distemper." The tone is that of an occasional poem designed to comfort her ailing husband. She uses a mock-heroic style to dignify the situation—for a husband afflicted with gout is no laughing matter—and concludes the poem with a tender, devoted, yet humorous address to her husband:

> For You my Dear whom late that pain did seize,
> Not rich enough to sooth the bad disease
> By large expences to engage his stay
> Nor yett so poor to fright the Gout away
> May you but some unfrequent Visits find
> To prove you patient, your Ardelia kind
> Who by a tender and officious care
> Will ease that Grief or her proportion bear
> Since Heaven does in the Nuptial state admitt
> Such cares but new endearments to begett
> And to allay the hard fatigues of life
> Gave the first Maid a Husband, Him a Wife.
> (pp. 31–32, ll. 51–62)

The personal basis for this fable marks it as unusual. For the most part Anne Finch adapted and embellished French sources. The fable gave scope to her gift for irony and her interest in moral improvement, and provided a varied convention within which human behavior, disguised by transposition into the animal kingdom or into a mythological setting, could be displayed in all its familiar freakiness, and wryly censured.

There is one fable composed by Anne Finch which suggests the strong attraction which the life of retirement held for her. "The Shepherd and the Calm" begins in a pastoral setting with a swain who, lured by a fantasy of adventure on the sea in its halcyon mood, "forsakes the Downs" for the rewards of life as a merchant voyager. He is the type of the malcontent, familiar in moral stories. The narrative is terse. His first voyage brings riches, his second, shipwreck. Cast up on the shores which he had rashly abandoned, he turns servant, "for small Profits . . . / Re-purchases in time th' abandon'd Sheep" and on a calm day, gazing at the ocean, delivers this panegyric to the retired life:

> Ev'n thus (quoth he) you seem'd all Rest and Ease,
> You sleeping Tempests, you untroubl'd Seas,
> That ne'er to be forgot, that luckless Hour,
> In which I put my Fortunes in your Pow'r;
> Quitting my slender, but secure Estate,
> My undisturb'd Repose, my sweet Retreat,
> For Treasures which you ravish'd in a Day,
> But swept my Folly, with my Goods, away.
> Then smile no more, nor these false Shews employ,
> Thou momentary Calm, thou fleeting Joy;
> No more on me shall these fair Signs prevail,
> Some other Novice may be won to Sail,
> Give me a certain Fate in the obscurest Vale.
>
> (pp. 184–85, ll. 46–58)

This "undisturb'd Repose" and "sweet Retreat," this "certain Fate in the ob-scurest Vale" is displayed and praised in those poems for which Anne Finch is best known: her poems of retirement.

The tradition to which the retirement poems belong has been examined at length by Maren-Sofie Røstvig in her two-volume study *The Happy Man,* and briefly by E. M. W. Tillyard in *Myth and the English Mind.* It is called the *beatus ille* or—not so appropriate for a woman poet—the *beatus vir* tradition. Røstvig identified Cowley as the central figure in the elaboration of the mode in English, in prose and verse, in the middle to late seventeenth century. The conception of character which pervades poems in this tradition emphasizes inner peace, self-mastery, freedom from slavery to the passions, mental independence, and emotional equilibrium. These virtues are associated with rural life, and the poems often explore a contrast between the affectation and corruption of court and city, and the calm beauty of country life. In Cowley, Anne Finch's model, Røstvig finds a strong, passionate strain of rejection of the world which is at odds with the stoical ideal at the source of the tradition. Anne Finch followed Cowley in this respect.[19]

In spite of its rejection of worldliness, including court life, the poetry of retirement was, in seventeenth-century England, a Royalist mode; in spite of its individualism and its sometimes passionate, enthusiastic advocacy of rural re-treat, it was anti-Puritan. Anne Finch's staunch support of the Stuart cause is apparent in her poetry as well as in the events of her life. She was a maid of honor at the Stuart court as a young woman, and she and her husband, an

Anglican nonjuror, lived in retirement after the parliamentary deposition of James II. Her political sympathies are shown in her poetry in her elegy "Upon the Death of King James the Second" and in "The Change," which describes the downfall of the Stuart dynasty in a series of moving emblems in the then-archaic convention of the Ruins of Time.

Like Cowley, Anne Finch lived in retirement by choice as a consequence of political loyalties. It is no doubt partly true, as Røstvig points out, that the elevation of retirement to an ideal choice of life was in part a manner of coping with political defeat by cutting losses, but Anne Finch found life away from court and city very suited to her temper and to her pursuit of poetry. In her prose preface to her manuscript poems, she reflects with satisfaction that she was not imprudent or vain enough to show her poetry to others while she lived at court, "where every one wou'd have made their remarks upon a Versifying Maid of Honour; and far the greater number with prejudice, if not contempt" (pp. 7–8). The apprehension of disparagement, she continues,

> had so much wean'd me from the practice and inclination to [poetry]; that had nott an utter change in my Condition, and Circumstances, remov'd me into the solitude, & security of the Country . . . I think I might have stopp'd . . . and suffer'd those few compositions I had then by me, to have sunk into . . . oblivion. . . . But when I came to Eastwell, and cou'd fix my eyes only upon objects naturally inspiring soft and Poeticall immaginations . . . I cou'd no longer keep within the limmitts I had pre-scrib'd myself. . . .
>
> (p. 8)

Her life at the family estate of the Earls of Winchilsea, where she and her husband found permanent refuge at the invitation of his nephew, the young Earl, turned her from a closet poet who feared the hostile scrutiny of self-styled critics to a poet who wrote habitually and openly. Under the judicious encouragement of her husband and other members of the family, she wrote the wide variety of poems which comprise her collected works. Many of the occasional pieces she wrote arise directly out of her associations with family and friends at other country estates, but the poems which are most intimately connected with her life in the country are the poems of retirement. Her poems in this vein show a rare concurrence of temperament, biography, and genre. This genre offered her as a woman poet a formal structure within which she could express in poetry her sense of herself as an outsider, an eccentric. The person in retirement is removed from the world and is deviant from its ways but is not an outcast because the fiction of reclusiveness honored in such poems is sanctioned by a long tradition.

The fragment "Enquiry After Peace" is a brief essay in the manner of the poems of retirement which goes astray because the poet gets lost in the details of the life of the world and cannot find her way back to the center of the poem. The poem begins with the question, "Peace! where art thou to be found?" (p. 67, l. 1), and stops, unfinished, with the lines, *"Poetry's the feav'rish Fit, / Th' o'erflowing of unbounded Wit"* (p. 68, ll. 40–41). It lacks context, focus and direction to give structure to the poet's invention.

"A Nocturnal Reverie," in contrast, is deftly focused by mood and occasion. It is composed firmly in a tradition of English poetry. It looks back to Shakespeare, from whom Anne Finch took the refrain "In such a night" which frames the poem; back to "Il Penseroso" and the concept of the melancholy temperament, which prefers night and solitude. It anticipates Young and Coleridge and the genre of Night Thoughts which came into prominence with the poets of sensibility and the Romantic poets. The "Reverie" is sustained in tone and structure, and the descriptive vignettes are at once graphic and stylized. It has a flawless coherence, its descriptive tableaux sensitively shaped to serve the ends of the poem. In a manner reminiscent of Charles Cotton's evening "Pastorals," she creates a mood by the accumulation of selected detail; sensuous, graphic, and evocative. Every image which has faded with the fading light has about it an apt and rich strangeness, and she expresses through details the frisson which we feel when, in the dark, we hear sounds which we cannot at once identify:

> When darken'd Groves their softest Shadows wear,
> And falling Waters we distinctly hear;
> When thro' the Gloom more venerable shows
> Some ancient Fabrick, awful in Repose,
> While Sunburnt Hills their swarthy Looks conceal,
> And swelling Haycocks thicken up the Vale:
> When the loos'd *Horse* now, as his Pasture leads,
> Comes slowly grazing thro' th' adjoining Meads,
> Whose stealing Pace, and lengthen'd Shade we fear,
> Till torn up Forage in his Teeth we hear. . . .
>
> (p. 269, ll. 23–32)

Toward the end of the poem there is a note which belongs to the "Il Penseroso" tradition, but which is rare in Anne Finch: the *o altitudo,* the dissolution into ecstasies:

> But silent Musings urge the Mind to seek
> Something, too high for Syllables to speak;

Till the free Soul to a compos'dness charm'd,
Finding the Elements of Rage disarm'd,
O'er all below a solemn Quiet grown,
Joys in th' inferiour World, and thinks it like her Own:
In such a *Night* let Me abroad remain,
Till Morning breaks, and All's confus'd again;
Our Cares, our Toils, our Clamours are renew'd,
Or Pleasures, seldom reach'd, again pursu'd.

(ll. 41–50)

She does not relinquish the old sense of hierarchy; the world of creatures is still inferior, though we may feel kinship with it and take joy in it, even prefer its composure to the confusions of diurnal human life. The free soul who delights in this world only "thinks it like her Own." To read into this passage, as Reynolds does, a new concept of nature as "a vital and separate entity" (p. cxxxi) is to ignore the qualifying word. The poet's empathy with the "shortliv'd Jubilee" of the creatures "whilst Tyrant-*Man* do's sleep" is poignantly expressed, but to call man a tyrant is to judge, not to dispute his authority. What Wordsworth noted and admired in this poem was the fresh attentiveness of the descriptive writing which suggests that "the eye of the Poet had been steadily fixed upon [her] object" and that her "feelings had urged [her] to work upon it in the spirit of genuine imagination" (p. lxxv). And it is true that a sense of something rare captivates the reader of this poem; it is almost uncannily moving. But the conventions of prosody and diction are decorously neoclassical, and the conceptual frame which sustains the poet's perceptions are in accord with the ideas of her age. Perhaps what enchants us in the text is the feeling it gives of a sensibility which is deviant without strain, which shines through conventions without disturbing them.

The central piece in Anne Finch's poems of retirement is "The Petition for an Absolute Retreat." As the poem says, the retreat must be "sweet, but absolute": sweet in the old sense of pure, unsullied, and absolute in its root sense, meaning "free." Two images, reiterated in the refrain, "those Windings and that Shade," dominate the poem: the maze or labyrinth, "Paths so lost . . . / That the World may ne'er invade"; and the shade or shelter, "Trees so high" that they provide both barrier and refuge, to preserve her "unshaken Liberty." In this kind of poem the ingredients are all prescribed by convention. Some may be included, some left out, but the test of the poet's handling of the genre is not in invention but in variation and choice of detail. Motifs are freely borrowed from other poets because the poem exists in all its richness only in the context of a known and established tradition. Thus in the third stanza Anne

Finch borrows and transforms details from Marvell's "The Garden" with another lending from the courtly love conceit that flowers grow where the beloved lady walks:

> Fruits indeed (wou'd Heaven bestow)
> All, that did in *Eden* grow,
> All, but the *Forbidden Tree,*
> Wou'd be coveted by me;
> Grapes, with Juice so crowded up,
> As breaking thro' the native Cup;
> Figs (yet growing) candy'd o'er,
> By the Sun's attracting Pow'r;
> Cherries, with the downy Peach,
> All within my easie Reach;
> Whilst creeping near the humble Ground,
> Shou'd the Strawberry be found
> Springing whereso'er I stray'd,
> Thro' those Windings and that Shade.
>
> (pp. 69–70, ll. 34–47)

There is some irony in the fact that a woman should be so at home in a convention called the *beatus vir* tradition—not that Anne Finch knew it by that name, but the aspirations which it expressed were firmly linked to one aspect of the classical masculine ideal. There are certain lines, however, that reveal the woman in the poet. The emotional force behind "Courteous Fate! afford me there / A *Table* spread without my Care," must gain from the fact that the passage was written by a woman who rebelled against the opinion that the "dull mannage of a servile house" was held by some "our outmost art, and use." The ideal of dress and deportment advanced in the poem finds its *locus classicus,* if not its source, in Ben Jonson's

> Give me a look, give me a face,
> That makes simplicity a grace;
> Robes loosely flowing, hair as free:
> Such sweet neglect more taketh me
> Than all the adulteries of art;

but Anne Finch's elaboration of the motif suggests a female bias:

> In the Fountains let me view
> All my Habit cheap and new;

63

> Such as, when sweet *Zephyrs* fly,
> With their Motions may comply;
> Gently waving, to express
> Unaffected Carelessness. . . .
> (ll. 66–71)

The passage on garments is embellished through some forty-five lines, including two extended similes. One of these figures, by invoking "the dear *Egyptian* Spouse," provides a link with and a clue to the next division of her theme. Here, by welcoming into her ideal retreat the moderate joys of married love, she follows a minor rather than the dominant strain in what was essentially an austere tradition:

> Give me there (since Heaven has shown
> It was not Good to be alone)
> A *Partner* suited to my Mind,
>
> . . . .
> When but Two the Earth possest,
> 'Twas their happiest Days, and best;
> They . . .
> Spent their own, and Nature's Prime,
> In Love; that only Passion given
> To perfect Man, whilst Friends with Heaven.
> (ll. 104–6, 112–13, 119–21)

The passage from "The Petition" quoted earlier makes it clear that Anne Finch had read Marvell's "The Garden" but, though he too invokes Paradise, he envisions there a solitary state:

> Such was that happy garden-state,
> While man there walked without a mate:
> . . . .
> Two Paradises 't'were in one
> To be in Paradise alone.
> (ll. 57–58, 63–64)

James Shirley is even surlier in his rejection of female companionship:

> No woman here shall find me out,
> Or if a chance do bring one hither,

I'll be secure, for round about
I'll moat it with my eyes foul weather.
    ("The Garden," ll. 29–32)

Although the amorous grove found a marginal place in the *beatus ille* tradition, celibacy, colored by misogyny, was central to it. This strain is linked with the traditional Christian association between women and primal depravity. The link between the poetry of pastoral retreat and celibacy is further reinforced by the fact that the *hortus conclusus* referred in courtly love convention to the intact virgin. There is in the poetry of retirement a regressive strain, suggested by the very word "retreat," and this strain can manifest itself in a longing for a pre-sexual state of innocence or a prehistorical golden age when celibacy reigned.

Anne Finch, however, wishes to take with her into retirement everything that gives her joy in life. Her poem is in part a celebration of what she most values. Although we know from other poems by her that she holds the orthodox view of women's responsibility in the Fall,

That since the Fall (by our seducement wrought)
Ours is the greater losse as ours the greater fault
    (p. 100, ll. 73–74)

she refuses to acquiesce in the matter of women's actual depravity, but staunchly holds to a view of compatible marriage as central to a complete and harmonious life.

Somewhat like her fables, the "Petition for an Absolute Retreat" describes a world which is diminished in scale, intelligible, and complete. But unlike the fables, which instruct us in how to be more sensible in this world, the "Petition" provides a kind of topography or anatomy of the ideal life in its completeness. The time spent in idyllic retirement is to be improved moment by moment in the contemplation of nature for "Thoughts of Pleasure, and of Use" (l. 129). This injunction is elaborated in a series of emblems of rivers and trees in the following lines which show how the natural scene can provide hieroglyphs for our spiritual and moral instruction. Though the reading of the Book of Nature unfolded in this passage is in keeping with the status of the whole "Petition" as an emblem of the spiritual life, Anne Finch's assurance in delineating natural images as correspondences places her sense of the natural world firmly in her own period. It is appropriate that she should in these lines echo George Herbert, who, along with Henry Vaughan, sustained together both the freshness of the perceived impression of the natural world and its emblematic significance.

The passage which echoes Herbert—or perhaps a common source in an emblem book—continues with the image of a vine, which is given immediate application not, like the preceding emblems, to the general human condition, but to Ardelia's own life narrative. The movement from desolation to rescue (which also provides a transition to the next theme in the poem) links the passage even more securely to the "turn" in Herbert's "The Flower":

> Who would have thought my shrivel'd heart
> Could have recover'd greennesse? It was gone
>   Quite under ground; as flowers depart
> To see their mother-root, when they have blown;
>   Where they together
>   All the hard weather,
>   Dead to the world, keep house unknown.
>
> (ll. 8–14)

The emblematic passage which parallels Herbert's "turn" briefly pulls into the poem the event which precipitated Anne Finch's life in retirement, and leads to the panegyric to friendship which follows:

> When a helpless Vine is found,
> Unsupported on the Ground,
> Careless all the Branches spread,
> Subject to each haughty Tread,
> Bearing neither Leaves, nor Fruit,
> Living only in the Root;
> Back reflecting let me say,
> So the sad *Ardelia* lay;
> Blasted by a Storm of Fate,
> Felt, thro' all the *British* State;
> Fall'n, neglected, lost, forgot,
> Dark Oblivion all her Lot;
> Faded till *Arminda's* Love,
> (Guided by the Pow'rs above)
> Warm'd anew her drooping Heart,
> And Life diffus'd thro' every Part. . . .
>
> (ll. 152–67)

The praise of friendship which ensues is not a digression but an integral part of a poem which honors those things which make up the complete life.

There is an interesting return, in the last lines of this passage, to the governing image of the retreat at the center of a labyrinth, protected by trees. The persona becomes identified with the retreat; she becomes the garden, the maze, and her heart the center, the quiet place:

> Give then, O indulgent Fate!
> Give a Friend in that Retreat
> (Tho' withdrawn from all the rest)
> Still a Clue, to reach my Breast.
> Let a Friend be still convey'd
> Thro' those Windings, and that Shade!
>   (ll. 196–201)

The identification of woman with garden is conventional courtly love iconography, but here in the context of friendship there are no erotic overtones. It is the "Breast," the soul or inner self, that is to be discovered by a friend who finds a clue to lead her through the windings and the shade.

We cannot with assurance answer the question of how deliberately Anne Finch devised her "Petition" as an emblem of the inner life, but certain arguments sustain this view. In Christian iconography the *hortus conclusus* is the soul, hence the analogy between garden and inner life or spirit would be allowable. Further, Anne Finch wrote other poems which show that expression through extended analogy was one of her habits of thought: "On Affliction," "Life's Progress," "The Change," "The Decision of Fortune," and "To a Fellow Scribbler."

As "The Petition" moves toward its close, the virtuous life which it describes is viewed from a higher perspective. The word "waste" at the beginning of the final section suggests a relinquishing of attachment to the goods of even a modest, virtuous life:

> Where, may I remain secure,
> Waste, in humble Joys and pure,
> A Life, that can no Envy yield;
> Want of Affluence my Shield.
>   (ll. 201–4)

This nuance of a suggestion that even a pure life is something to be wasted or used up withdraws ultimate value from it and prepares us for the conclusion which involves, as in "Il Penseroso," a movement toward transcendence:

> But as those, who Stars wou'd trace
> From a subterranean Place,
> Through some Engine lift their Eyes

67

To the outward, glorious Skies;
So th' immortal Spirit may,
When descended to our Clay,
From a rightly govern'd Frame
View the Height, from whence she came;
To her Paradise be caught,
And things unutterable taught.
Give me then, in that Retreat,
Give me, O indulgent Fate!
For all Pleasures left behind,
Contemplations of the Mind.

(ll. 270–83)

She is very precise about the conditions for illumination: the height from which the immortal spirit came can be seen only from a "rightly govern'd Frame." The grounds for rapture can be cultivated at the still center; "all Heaven" can "be survey'd / From those Windings and that Shade" (ll. 292–93). This elaborate gesture toward the transcendent which concludes the poem perfects the delineation of the complete life which is its substance.

The "Petition for an Absolute Retreat" is a fine example of how Anne Finch, a woman writing, adapted a masculine tradition, the *beatus vir*, to her own conception of the life of contentment: the *beata femina*. Some forms developed with the dominant sex in mind can be gracefully adapted, transformed, and embellished by women writers to suit their purposes, which are often oblique or slant toward the tradition which the form embodies. Some time-honored fictions, however, are not so tractable. In the English, Christian tradition in which Anne Finch wrote, certain major stories and institutions stand at the very center of literature. What is a woman writer to make of them in her work? For a devout Christian poet like Anne Finch, the attitude toward canonical Christian myths is clear. We have seen from her asides about "female Clay" and "the weaker kinde" that she acquiesced in the doctrinal version of the story of the Fall. She does protest in "The Introduction" that women are "Education's, more then Nature's fools," and in one poem there is a tone of bewildered lament in her itemizing of men's prerogatives. The panegyric at the conclusion of "A Poem, Occasion'd by the Sight of the 4th Epistle Lib. Epist: 1. of Horace" quickly turns from its subject, the glories of male poets and their translators, to the plight of the sex to which the woman writing the panegyric belongs. The self-deprecation in this complimentary closing can be seen as part of the convention in which such a poem is written, but the force of the lines suggests that they are heartfelt:

Anne Finch

Happy You three! happy the Race of Men!
Born to inform or to correct the Pen
To proffitts pleasures freedom and command
Whilst we beside you but as Cyphers stand
T' increase your Numbers and to swell th' account
Of your delights which from our charms amount
And sadly are by this distinction taught
That since the Fall (by our seducement wrought)
Ours is the greater losse as ours the greater fault.

(p. 100, ll. 63–73)

Classical mythology, however, was not sacrosanct. Its stories were clearly fictions; they had nothing to do with virtue and salvation. For this very reason, they provide an opportunity for a playful tone, as in "The Circuit of Appollo" and "Mercury and the Elephant." Her "The Answer (To Pope's *Impromptu*)" takes a fiction from classical mythology which is usually invoked in a context of high seriousness, as at the end of Milton's "Lycidas," and uses it in playful warning:

You of one Orpheus sure have read,
  Who would like you have writ
Had he in London town been bred,
  And polish'd to[o] his wit;
But he poor soul thought all was well,
  And great should be his fame,
When he had left his wife in hell,
  And birds and beasts could tame.
Yet venturing then with scoffing rhimes
  The women to incense,
Resenting Heroines of those times
  Soon punished his offence. .
And as the Hebrus roll'd his scull,
  And harp besmear'd with blood,
They clashing as the waves grew full,
  Still harmoniz'd the flood.
But you our follies gently treat,
  And spin so fine the thread,
You need not fear his awkward fate,
  The lock wo'n't cost the head.

(p. 103, ll. 9–28)

Her comic treatment of the Orphic myth deflates the figure of Orpheus to the status of a poor husband who thought, after abandoning his wife in hell, that he was well and truly rid of women, but found to his sorrow that incensed women became "Resenting Heroines" who pursued him to an ignominious end. The bantering tone of this poem is appropriate to its context: an exchange of compliments between Pope and Anne Finch after the publication of *The Rape of the Lock.*

As well as a treasury of stories and repertory of forms, literary tradition provides a poet with images which have gathered certain connotations through long use in poetry. A poet can either reinforce or alter the traditional associations of such an image. One traditional image which recurs in the poems of Anne Finch is the image of the bird.[20]

The bird is a very old emblem in English poetry. It has a range of signification as wide as that of any of the old, central images in our literature: harbinger of spring, figure of the transience of life, embodiment of freedom, symbol of the singer and poet. In Anne Finch's poetry, the bird often occurs in figures of speech about herself. At the end of the brief reflective lyric "On Myselfe," she writes,

> When in the Sun, my wings can be display'd,
> And in retirement, I can bless the shade.
>
> (p. 15, ll. 11–12)

The self in the metaphor of a bird in these lines is subject to weather which she does not create but to which she can accommodate herself: an adaptable, undemanding creature, who at best accepts what circumstances bring, but does not initiate. In the emblematic "The Consolation" (p. 18), the "soaring Lark," who flies in the sun's beams "As if she never thought of a return," is an exemplum of the unfailing rhythm of our lives. At night she must fall to earth, but when "the swift hand of time / Renews the morning" she will soar again. She is an emblem of hope or of the grounds of hope in reasonable expectation. This bird is generically human, with no apparent personal associations.

In the complimentary poem "To Mr. Prior From a Lady Unknown" (p. 102), Anne Finch compares herself to a "fond bird," expending his life to "raise his mimic throat" in "little art." Whether this poem can be taken as her serious assessment of her poetic powers is questionable, because the complimentary poem requires a belittling of the apprentice who is paying the compliment. "The Bird" (pp. 265–66) begins with an enumeration of the qualities of the bird, who is to be immortalized through praise. The poem moves through a contrast between freedom and constraint, a contrast very common in Anne

70

Finch's poems. The bird in this poem is captive; he sings "domestick musick." His captivity is pictured as shelter, and as a renunciation of the false allurements of wanton love. The little narrative of the poem is about the bird's reform. He will never return to the woods, the poet says, but she enjoins him not to mourn his "wild freedom." He has found a secure shelter next to her heart where he will do her the kind office of warning her of the approach of false love. The poem is about taming: the taming of a wild bird associated with love, and by inference the taming of desire. At another level, it may be a rejection of the conventions of erotic poetry: the bird in his wild state had graced the mischief of love with a song, and rejoiced over the misery of fallen lovers. Anne Finch wrote many tender poems about married love, but she does not celebrate in her poetry the amoral Eros who looks with indifference on the wretchedness of lovers. "The Bird" is in a sense a hieroglyph of her life as a poet. The bird as songster is traditionally an emblem of poetic inspiration. By domesticating it, she confines its range of flight and song, but purifies it of the vanities of false love.

Anne Finch's poem "To the Nightingale" (pp. 267–68) has been sensitively analyzed by Ann Messenger in her essay "Selected Nightingales and an 'Augustan' Sensibility,"[21] She sees in it an adroit mingling of convention and confession, of metaphysical, Augustan, and Romantic motifs and stylistic devices. She traces the movement of the poem from the aspiration in its opening similes to the rapture of its middle section, to its wise yet rueful conclusion. Thus, like many of Anne Finch's poems, "To the Nightingale" moves from aspiration to resignation. By describing the soaring music of the bird, she participates in it, but her stated lot is doubly different. She ends by first reproving the bird for its neglect of life's business and then ruefully commenting on the convention of moralizing that she, being human, has fallen into.

In these poems are found various permutations of the bird image: the bird as subject to inner and outer weather; as a fond pupil imitating her master's model song; as a tamed and transformed accomplice of the god of love; as a model of ecstatic song who serves to recall to us our human limitations. The doubleness of the bird image as this poet uses it is related to the tension that sustains her poetry: between bold aspiration and humility, between society and solitude, between wildness and restraint. The poems suggest that she identifies not with the bird in its wild ecstatic strain but with the bird confined, domesticated and reformed.

But her description of the bird in its "wild freedom" suggests a sympathy with it which is expressed most powerfully in her narrative poem "The Bird and the Arras." This poem is about the panic in imprisonment of a creature by nature wild. It can be argued that the images of the bird and the arras are used with a resonance which arises from her sense of women's place in culture. We have already noted in the long poem describing the tapestries at Longleat that she mourned the loss to women of the art of weaving in which they once excelled but which men have now usurped, relegating women to the trivial handiwork which she rejected in her lines from "The Spleen." In "The Bird and the Arras" the bird is shut out from the seeming paradise in the arras. It is tempting to see the imprisoned and excluded bird as an emblem of the predicament of women contained by social restraints and excluded from art, but such a reading cannot be insisted on because it comes from a twentieth-century point of view. In late-seventeenth-century terms, the poem can be read simply as an emblem of the general human predicament: we are trapped in this life, shut out from paradise. The arras, an inviting grove, is a *hortus conclusus*. It looks like Eden but it cannot be entered.

The movement from imprisonment to freedom in the poem reverses the usual pattern found in Anne Finch's poetry. The poem is an exploration of *trompe l'oeil*, the deceptiveness of appearances; its governing figure is irony, Anne Finch's favorite trope. The crisis in the tale occurs when the bird, aspiring to mount higher than the birds pictured in the tapestry, is dashed to the ground. The rapid, terse narrative displays the poet's virtuoso command of the rhymed couplet:

> By neer resemblance see that Bird betray'd
> Who takes the well wrought Arras for a shade
> There hopes to pearch and with a chearfull Tune
> O're-passe the scortchings of the sultry Noon.
> But soon repuls'd by the obdurate scean
> How swift she turns but turns alas in vain
> That piece a Grove, this shews an ambient sky
> Where immitated Fowl their pinnions ply
> Seeming to mount in flight and aiming still more high.
> All she outstrip's and with a moments pride
> Their understation silent does deride
> Till the dash'd Cealing strikes her to the ground
> No intercepting shrub to break the fall is found
> Recovering breath the window next she gaines
> Nor fears a stop from the transparent Panes.
>
> (p. 51, ll. 1–15)

There is a kind of unexplained hiatus in the text at this point, then a brief, graphic elaboration of the bird's terror, followed by an abrupt ending, the *deus ex machina* of rescuing human hands:

But we degresse and leave th' imprison'd wretch
Now sinking low now on a loftyer stretch
Flutt'ring in endlesse cercles of dismay
Till some kind hand directs the certain way
Which through the casement an escape affoards
And leads to ample space the only Heav'n of Birds.

(ll. 16–21)

The final line qualifies the bird image as emblem of the human predicament. The human soul has other spiritual homes.[22]

Yet the reader leaves this poem with a sense that its subject is emblematic of the poet who was moved to write it. Such an interpretation is strengthened by a reading of another poem placed early in Anne Finch's poems, "Fragment." This poem, noted earlier as a kind of progress of the soul, tells a narrative about Ardelia, Anne Finch's persona, who, "confin'd, and but to female Clay," "mistook the rightful Way" (p. 13, ll. 1–2). Then the "flaming Sword" of the Stuarts' dethronement pitches the ruling powers to wreck and ruin, in which Ardelia shares, "With them thrown prostrate to the humble Ground" (l. 15). Instructed by her fall, Ardelia withdraws her desires and aspirations from the delusions of this world and turns her thoughts to "a more certain Station" (l. 18). The poem counsels resignation, yet the lines describing the things which must be renounced are alluring:

But all in vain are Pray'rs, extatick Thoughts,
Recover'd Moments, and retracted Faults,
Retirement, which the World *Moroseness* calls,
Abandon'd Pleasures in Monastick Walls. . . .

(ll. 21–24)

The concluding lines describing the heaven to which the soul, chastened by disillusionment, must aspire, contain some wonderful touches in the old Metaphysical manner, which the poet naturally turns to when her subject is religious devotion:

Th' Expanse, the Light, the Harmony, the Throng,
The Bride's Attendance, and the Bridal Song,
The numerous Mansions, and th' immortal Tree,
No Eye, unpurg'd by Death, must ever see. . . .

(ll. 32–35)

It is apparent that the movement traced in small in "The Bird and the Arras," from aspiration, to delusion, to ruin, to realization, is traced in the larger pattern of Ardelia's life in "Fragment." It must be said that the pattern from vanity in placing false hopes in the semblances of the world to a realization of the error of this way is a truism of the moral and spiritual life understood from Christian instruction; it says nothing about Anne Finch's womanhood. Yet the sense of extremity in both poems, the passion of the gestures of aspiration and the plummeting to ruin, are part of Anne Finch's whole sensibility, and the ironic narrative of both these poems is also the narrative of her poetic career, from aspiration, to dejection at the ridicule of the world, to the consolation of cultivating a modest muse and of knowing that the judgments of the world are vain.

It seems appropriate to conclude by stepping back to gain a wider perspective on Anne Finch's poems, and to state in what their abiding interest lies: her resourcefulness in adapting the poetic conventions of her day to her own designs. She used those conventions to contain and express both her vulnerability and her keen awareness of her oblique relationship to the literary tradition, as a woman writer.

John Goode, in "Women and the Literary Text," says that the text is a "project realized within determined circumstances which limit the questions it can ask, give it *margins* which rule it off from that about which it is compelled to be silent."[23] Literary and social decorum in Anne Finch's time constituted highly determined circumstances which limited the questions a lady could ask, the answers a lady could hazard. In reading Anne Finch one has to remember her gentility—tempered though it may be by her wit, her melancholy waywardness, and her good sense. Her poetic speech is always the speech of a lady. "Ardelia to Melancholy" is as close as she comes to confession, and in it she speaks through her pastoral persona. The brief, moving poem "To Death" is marked by a restraint and self-effacement which manifest her desire for seemliness as well as her Christian piety. Even in anticipating her own death, her main concern is for others.

Within the circumstances of class, religion, gender, temperament, and fate, she determinedly wrote poetry. She was not formally inventive, nor did she show mastery of any one form. She used what was at hand. She chose not to write satire, the dominant mode of her day. She explored flexible—and by her time already outmoded--forms like the Pindaric ode and the reverie. From the conventions of pastoral she borrowed the device of poetic names like Ardelia and Dafnis around which she could elaborate a literary fiction which expressed her love of the countryside, and through which she could address to her husband love poems which establish her adroitness in aligning herself with the conventions of a tradition of love poetry older than and different from the ones which prevailed in her day. The persona, Ardelia, also provided her on many poetic occasions with the distance which she or the poem required. She felt at home in private occasional poems to particular persons; these allowed the decorous expression of personal feeling and provided an opportunity for description and the play of wit within the bounds of affection and respect. The fable she loved because it allowed embellishment of a given narrative in the service of good conduct and permitted the use of a familiar tone and the introduction of picturesque domestic detail in the interest of story. Because it was new, it was not a genre which caused her to look with anxiety to the example of others who had already done much better than she feared she was likely to do. In the poem of retirement she found a genre which suited her temper, her fate and life circumstances, and her position as a woman writer marginal to the literary institutions of her time. Some of her most moving poems are composed around the image of the bird, which seemed for her to capture in small the complex of associations which expressed her sense of herself as a poet and woman. When this happens she is able to invest a seemingly slight occasion—a small bird trapped in a tapestried room—with a passion which gives symbolic resonance to a brief poem. Sometimes, as we have seen, she adopts an ironic or mock-heroic tone to provide a new slant on an old story or to bridge the distance between occasion and poetic convention. This she does with great inventiveness and humor in "Upon Ardelia's Return Home" (pp. 24–27). This ladylike romp is a virtuoso piece of great charm. It recounts with picturesque detail how, lured by her Muse to stray too far from home, she appeals to Phoebus first for his chariot, and, when refused, for his "winged steed." Apollo replies that Pegasus would be disgraced by having a female on his back, but if she will be content with a mere "conveniency," she could return home in a plain English water-cart. This she does in fine style, "Exalted high to all beholders," a nice burlesque of the rescued maiden. Upon her homecoming she turns her predicament and its comic solution into verse, turning it to "Poetick Glory." Like so many of her poems, this piece traces the movement from straying "By the aluring Muse betray'd" to homecoming. Her plight is real: poetic fancies have led her too far in her ramblings and she had no mind to take "Cold earth and boughs" "for Bed and Cover." Its resolution is comic in its recognition of the amusing figure she must cut, but she never loses her poise. The whole poem plays, through burlesque, on the notion that women must be both compliant and resourceful in making do with second best.

The poem can be read as a playful commentary on her relation as a woman poet to literature. Her vocation is undeniable: she has been following her Muse. If she cannot ride on the high horse reserved for male poets, she will, unfazed, adapt to this deprivation by accommodating herself to a lesser vehicle, and turning her very disadvantage, including humiliation, into poetry. In a sense, "Upon Ardelia's Return Home" is her way of explaining to herself, through her own inventive fancy, how she persisted in remaining a poet in spite of discouragement.

The renewed interest in Anne Finch among contemporary women poets and critics makes it clear that she is a precursor, even an exemplar, for women writers. It is now possible to see her work in relation to a larger whole which is only now becoming visible, thanks to the work of women editors and critics: the traditions of women's literature. A reading of her complete work in this new context fleshes her out into a resourceful, dedicated, and skilled poet whose flashes of brilliance are sustained by the habitual writing of poetry in a wide variety of genres. She persistently turned the associations, circumstances, and occasions of her life into poems which, like "Upon Ardelia's Return Home," made poetry out of her predicament, and bridged the distance between the conventions of poetry and her position as a woman poet, with poems which made new fictions out of her exclusion from the old.

Presumptuous Poetess, Pen-Feathered Muse:

THE COMEDIES OF MARY PIX

JULIET MCLAREN

Or could I write like the two Female things,
With Muse Pen-feathered, guiltless yet of Wings;
And yet, it strives to Fly, and thinks it Sings.
Just like the Dames themselves, who flaunt in Town,
And flutter loosely, but to tumble down.
(*Animadversions on Mr. Congreve's Late Answer to Mr. Collier*)

Aphra Behn is the first English woman known to have earned her living by writing for the stage, but she was by no means the last in her century. Within seven years of her death, five more women had written plays for the London stage and three of those five, Delariviere Manley, Catharine Trotter, and Mary Pix, would go on to have moderately successful literary careers during the next decade. Two of those who attempted plays during this time—"Ariadne" and "A Young Lady"—were perhaps too timid, or may have been, like Anne Finch, of too elevated a social class to court anything like a serious career in the theatrical world; their first attempts at play-writing seem to have been their last. But the others were entirely serious in their efforts and persevered against ridicule and censure in an attempt to learn their craft. They wrote sometimes with the support of sympathetic men, often against considerable male opposition and opprobrium, and from a perspective on the situation of women that I would define as feminist, however they may have differed from one another in background or education.

The initial opportunity for these women came as the result of the dissolution of the United Theatre Company into two rival companies in the winter of

1694–95. Thomas Betterton, the leading actor of his day, and a number of other rebellious performers broke away from the United Company at the Drury Lane Theatre to reopen the Lincoln's Inn Fields Theatre, taking with them not only the company's most experienced actors, but also its most popular scripts. The actors were in flight from a penny-pinching and perhaps dishonest theater manager, and this flight marked the beginning of a decade of intense rivalry between the theaters.[1]

With both groups of actors hungry for new plays and competing for a relatively scanty audience, women interested in writing for the public could have their theatrical efforts accepted and produced. The novices began by offering plays to the now-struggling company at Drury Lane, but even their modest efforts aroused the competitive hostility of young male actors in the company who also fancied themselves as playwrights and critics. This hostility culminated in the viciously funny misogynist satire, *The Female Wits*, produced in 1696 at the Theatre Royal, Drury Lane.[2] The anonymously authored farce temporarily silenced two of the new writers—Delariviere Manley and Catharine Trotter—and sent the third, Mary Pix, to offer her services as a writer to Betterton's troupe at Lincoln's Inn Fields. But in spite of this attack, these women's success in their efforts was sufficient to encourage others to join them during the next few years. In fact, one of these later women playwrights, Susanna Centlivre, was to become one of the most successful comic dramatists of the eighteenth century.

While the new women writers attempted both comedy and tragedy, it is in comedy—so often the medium for social comment, both open and covert—with its traditional focus on love, courtship, and marriage, that their particular and sometimes radical ideas about the nature of women and the relations between men and women can most easily be seen. It is, after all, marriage which is the central experience for most women in any society, and it is within marriage that the real issues of power, freedom, and women's economic security must be resolved. The major decision about her life which a young woman of the late seventeenth century might hope to have the freedom to make for herself was the choice of a husband, while widows had to decide whether to give up their relative freedom—and to whom—in a second marriage. Since a widow would lose control of her jointure and whatever else she had inherited to her second husband, but without a husband was often dominated by some close male relative, the issue was not a simple one.[3] And even the most conventionally reared woman would be more likely than in an earlier century to consider these questions, since love and marriage were the metaphors into which the rhetoric of revolution and the definition of the civil contract had been translated over and over again during the preceding three generations. As Susan Staves describes it in her discussion of this issue:

For people who thought in terms of the hierarchical ordering of the great chain of being, the relations of sovereigns and subjects were analogous to the relations of parents and children and of husbands and wives. . . . Because the traditional analogies between sovereign/subject relations and domestic relations persisted in the late seventeenth century, the dilemmas of sovereign/subject relations . . . inevitably affected contemporary thought about authority and obligation in the family. The same questions that had been raised about the absolute authority of the king [in seventeenth-century England] were now raised about the absolute authority of fathers and husbands. . . . After rebellion became respectable at the Glorious Revolution, such questions were asked with increasing seriousness.[4]

Unfortunately, few of the early efforts of these play-writing women have reached our time in modern editions; fewer still have been read and discussed for either their merits or their intentions. Scholarly work in the texts of a past age tends to follow the dominant model of male scholarship and male reading, particularly in a period where until quite recently there have been only male texts. And it has been a critical assumption of long standing that the fledgling authors in petticoats were somehow attempting nothing more than copies of masculine literary genres and not doing that particularly well.[5] A reexamination of this notion is overdue, for on the evidence of their texts many of these early writers can be defined as consciously feminist in their intentions.[6] Most of the female playwrights were choosing to present characters and events in their plays from a perspective different from that of their male peers and associates, in spite of the difficult task of pleasing the critics—who were often their rivals—and the audiences of the day.

Nancy Cotton discusses the origins of the traditional, dismissive critical bias against women authors, the "Salic Law of Wit," and its effect on women writing in the seventeenth century in the last two chapters of her survey, *Women Playwrights in England c. 1363–1750*.[7] She points out that women writing in this century were consistently criticized by their male contemporaries for being both females and unnatural. She quotes from a seventeenth-century example, *A Journal from Parnassus*:

> Apollo seeing a body of a more than female size wrapt up in Hoods & Petticoats . . . was about to appoint a Committee of Muses to examine her Sex: . . . in short, since her Works had neither Witt enough for Man, nor Modesty enough for a Woman, she was to be look'd upon as an Hermaphrodite, & consequently not fit to enjoy the Benefits and Priviledges of either Sex, much less of this Society.[8]

To be fair, one must add that hostility and defamation were general, but not universal. Charles Gildon's continuation of Langbaine's *Lives and Characters of the English Dramatick Poets* (1699) often praises women writers, as does Giles Jacob in his *Poetical Register* (1719).[9] Such nineteenth-century theater historians as John Genest (1832) and Dr. John Doran (1847) are also generous to "the Ladies," Doran giving women playwrights from Aphra Behn to Susanna Centlivre a complimentary chapter of their own in his *Annals of the English Stage*.[10] Unfortunately, these instances of acknowledgment were relatively few.

Criticism during the past thirty-five years, particularly that by women scholars, has generally been more inclusive, but with one or two exceptions has not addressed the feminism of the late seventeenth and early eighteenth centuries. Some recent studies, such as that by Margaret L. McDonald, *The Independent Woman in the Restoration Comedy of Manners*,[11] fail to discuss women's plays to any significant degree, concentrating instead on the representation of women in plays written by men. Fidelis Morgan's anthology of women's plays from this early period, *The Female Wits: Women Playwrights on the London Stage, 1660–1720*, does an initial service in rescuing some lost or little-known plays of the time from obscurity and presenting them in modern dress.[12] But her introductions are necessarily brief and concentrate primarily on biographies of these women so long ignored by scholarship. She has also omitted the contemporary prologues and epilogues which often reveal the feelings of the writers about their audiences and their critical reception. Even such an original and scholarly study of the Restoration and post-Restoration theater as Susan Staves's *Players' Sceptres*, which examines many issues from the women's point of view, generally fails to comment on distinctions between male and female playwrights' versions of love, marriage, and the moral nature of women in the plays of the period.[13]

Exceptions to this general climate of omission would include the work done in the 1950s by Jean Gagen, *The New Woman: Her Emergence in English Drama, 1600–1730*, in which (for example) she contrasts the treatment given to the female virtuoso in Susanna Centlivre's *The Basset Table* and the free-ranging satires on learned women created by male authors of the same period.[14] Gagen observes in her discussion of women writers that *"these* women—these Mrs. Behns, Mrs. Manleys, Mrs. Pixes and Mrs. Cockburns and the rest—were not only airing their opinions freely but brazenly rivalling men in one of the toughest of professions. And harder to bear was the fact that some of them were doing it with a disconcerting success."[15] A more recent essay is Edna Steeves's introduction to the reprint edition of the plays of two of these post-Restoration writers, Mary Pix and Catharine Trotter (Mrs. Cockburn), in which she refers to Pix and her contemporary, Delariviere Manley, as feminist writers.[16] Steeves's work in preparing the facsimile reprint edition of the plays of two of these women has the added benefit of making their plays available to modern readers for the first time.[17] In the 1970s, Paula Louise Barbour prepared a critical edition of one of Mrs. Pix's comedies and later wrote a paper on her. [18] While neither of these efforts has been published so far as I am aware, they have been drawn upon by Constance Clark in *Three Augustan Women Playwrights* (1986), in which she discusses Mary Pix, Catharine Trotter, and Delariviere Manley. [19] Clark's study of these three writers emphasizes their lives and their early writing for the theater. That is, her work examines those productions which prompted *The Female Wits*, but while extremely valuable and well documented, it is an initial analysis of a few texts rather than a complete study.

Even with these exceptions to the general silence about the women playwrights who saw themselves as successors and heirs to Aphra Behn, too little attention has been paid to their struggles and their achievements. To address and correct a portion of this imbalance I wish to examine several comedies written by Mary Pix, whose literary career spanned the years between 1695 and 1707, to discover what effect the theatrical situation of her time had on her career and how she responded in her plays to the social attitudes toward women expressed by the men of her world. She is typical in some ways of the early women playwrights: in her modesty, her sensitivity to criticism, her sense of isolation and struggle as a woman writer, her friendships with other writing women. But her plays represent ways in which she is unique and rather remarkable for her time. As Steeves writes:

> [Pix] was a feminist before feminism became trendy. Although not stridently offensive in her feminism, as her contemporary Mrs. Manley could be, she seizes every opportunity to defend women against attacks upon their character and intelligence. And like her near contemporaries, Mrs. Manley and Mrs. Trotter, Mrs. Pix by her success as a playwright served as a model for other women aspiring to write for the stage.
>
> (p. xlviii)

Steeves concludes, "the impact of her plays, and the support given by her success to the general history of feminism and women's rights long before those terms took on their modern connotation, is not an insubstantial one" (p. liv). So far she is the only critic to have pointed this out. I believe that Pix's attempts to write the truth of her situation appear in the plays, prologues, and poems she created. Through her, all these writing women stand before us, perhaps for the first time, not as the dull inventors of "wishy-washy stuff," [20] but with the boldness enunciated by one of her successors, Eliza Haywood, in the prologue to her comedy, *A Wife to be Lett*: "Criticks! be dumb tonight—no Skill display; / A dangerous *Woman-Poet* wrote the Play!" [21]

In her second play and first attempt at comedy, *The Spanish Wives* (1696), written for the Patent Company at the Drury Lane Theatre, [22] Mary Pix addresses the issues of freedom and obedience within marriage from the wives' point of view. Like many other comedies of the decade, *The Spanish Wives* concerns already married couples. As Staves points out, comedies from the seventies and eighties onward, while still using marriage itself as a device for closure, are increasingly likely to "begin with major characters already married"; she also suggests that "these characters are more likely to represent problems [within the marriage] than to be the simple butts of humor they tend to be in the earlier comedies."[23] The long-standing custom of setting potentially controversial plays in foreign places, frequently used in tragedy to disguise political comment and circumvent censorship, [24] makes the "Spanish farce" a natural choice for a novice with an audience of uncertain temper to please. Pix also plays on contemporary ideas of the "Spanish" husband, that is, someone who is unreasonably jealous, and the "Spanish virgin," that is, someone who by virtue of being kept in confinement is extraordinarily passionate.[25]

Pix creates a stock double plot revolving around two married women who are attempting to change the rules by which they are governed. One couple is an old husband / young wife pair; the wife is restless, as is traditional, and has an "English" beau. She is married to the Governor of Barcellona [sic] who is not at all a "Spanish" husband, that is, he gives "his Wife more Liberty than is usual in Spain" (dramatis personae).[26] They address one another with the crude endearments usually put in the mouths of "cits" in Restoration comedies, calling each other "Tittup" and "Dearie," which underlines (perhaps) their commitment to "Whiggish" liberty and suggests the old Governor's plebian origins—libertarians at this time often being of the lower middle class. Unlike many similar May-December marriages, theirs is a reasonably contented one as long as the Governor is so amiable and easygoing. He is contrasted also to the jealous and usually cuckolded London husband of his type in other plays: unlike them, he assumes that his wife's amusements are harmless. It is almost as if the author has concocted an argument from her sympathy for women to explain his attitudes.

The other couple, the Marquess of Moncada and Elenora, are not happy; he is the "Spanish" husband and she the "Spanish" wife, a virtual prisoner. The two men discuss their opposing views of marriage and women's fidelity in the opening scene. The Governor is opposed to jealousy and believes in trusting his wife and giving her freedom in the "English" fashion (I, pp. 1–3); the Marquess believes all women to be faithless and thinks the Governor is a naive fool. Pix puts the argument for jealousy in the mouth of a character who turns out to be both unpleasant and evil; she puts the argument for tolerance (indeed for cuckoldry) in the mouth of the dear old Governor: "Pough! I have been in England. There they are the happiest husbands. If a man does happen to be a

Cuckold, which by the way is almost as rare as in Spain, but I say if it does fall out, all his Wife's Friends are his" (I, p. 2). The author disappoints the audience's expectation of a standard Restoration comedy betrayal scene, however, as the Governor is not cuckolded after all, even though the Marquess manages to arouse the Governor's jealousy to such a degree that he finally threatens to lock his Lady up. She promptly retaliates with a threat of her own: "Do! Lock me up, and next moment you are gone, I'll hang myself in my own Garters, so I will. Can you behold your Tittup hang'd? Her eyes goggling, her mouth you have bussed so often, gaping, and her legs dangling three yards above Ground?" (III, p. 41). Shocked by her threat, the Governor relents and they arrange a sensible compromise.

That a wife's choices are extremely limited in this situation is also made clear by the Lady's relationship with her English lover. For charming though he may be, he has no honorable intentions: "I should scarce accept the Governor's wife for mine, if he would give her. But I am amorous and eager, as Love and Beauty can inspire hot and vigorous youth" (III, p. 28). The wife is saved from the foolishness of adultery by her husband, who sees through her attempt to spend time alone with the Englishman and circumvents her. He reverses the Marquess's sneering judgment of him as a fool for being complacent, while the insanely jealous Marquess fails to see through a plot for his unhappy wife's rescue, in spite of his suspicious nature. When his wife has been taken beyond his reach, he goes off stage raving, while the governor's wife says, " 'Tis a just judgment on him Deary for being so jealous," and her husband rather drily observes, "Ay, Tittup, when Women never give any cause you know, Tittup" (III, p. 45). The Lady then volunteers to tell her English Colonel not to see her again; when she does so, to show *his* generosity her husband offers to leave both his wife and his money to the Colonel, "about Threescore years hence" (III, p. 48). The Governor and his Lady have agreed to "deal together" at last with honesty and mutual trust: she to remain faithful, he to allow her social freedom. Obedience for her is shown to derive from a contract, a mutual agreement within a legally binding marriage. This effort to arrange a workable, if not idyllic, relationship, based on shared rights, is apparently the function of these characters within the farce.

The other marriage is quite different. The Marquess of Moncada has no interest in his beautiful wife except as property. She is kept in close confinement, unable to receive even female visitors except on rare occasions. Moncada is portrayed as a cowardly bully whose principal techniques in dealing with women are coercion and threat, extending even to physical brutality. He is not above using hired thugs to enforce his will. The Governor is uneasy about Moncada's tyranny over his wife, but accepts it as his legal right, until Moncada causes a domestic uproar for the Governor himself. At that point the older man loses his temper: "Go thy ways for a troublesome, maggot-pated, jealous-crowned simpleton, as thou art!" (II, p. 26), is the Governor's rebuke, prompted by irritation rather than moral concern. Depictions of a battered wife or even implicit arguments against the wife being her husband's property are not usual in comedy; they would perhaps be more acceptable to general audiences if the scene were Barcelona rather than London. And the sympathy that is extended to Elenora comes from another married women. Unlike the easygoing Governor, his Lady is furious about Elenora's situation and resolves to do what she can to help the unfortunate woman escape with her somewhat passive lover, Camillus. She sends her own maid, Spywell, to concoct an intrigue with Elenora's maid, Orada, and with Hidewell, Camillus's clever servant. They discover amusing ways to send hidden messages and to mislead the Marquess, who, suspecting an intrigue, plans to take his wife into hiding. Orada devises a rescue plot, and Camillus, Hidewell, and a comic friar who attends Camillus waylay the coach containing the unhappy wife and rescue her. Once again Pix disappoints the audience, who are conditioned to expect infidelity by the long tradition of Restoration comedy (and she knows it may cause her trouble; her epilogue is somewhat defensive): the Spanish wife is not overwhelmed by passion, but remains resolutely virtuous. In both speech and action she refuses adultery or indeed any behavior that might compromise her sense of propriety. The denouement reveals that her marriage to Moncada is invalid; she was precontracted to Camillus before Moncada kidnapped her with the connivance of her greedy family.

In this play Mary Pix structures the first of the alliances among women which will appear in all her comedies. The Governor's Lady feels as responsible and concerned for Elenora's freedom as for her own; she is interested in Elenora's welfare as a guest in her home and as another married woman caught in an unhappy situation. There is no rivalry between them over a man and there are no genuinely immoral women in the play, only immoral, cowardly, or incompetent men: the Marquess, who has stolen Elenora and who flees when Camillus tries to fight him; the English colonel, who tries to seduce the governor's wife; and Friar Andrew, the Spanish friar who is described as lecherous, faithless to his vows, overly fond of drink, and a pimp. (He also falls off ladders and is afraid of the dark and of heights; Pix makes him the butt of contemporary anti-Catholic feeling.)

The comic structure and character development of the piece are far from complex. The experience of the actors in the Drury Lane company was very limited and their numbers were small. But however slight, as a play written for the Patent Company in the first year after Thomas Betterton and Elizabeth Barry's departure had to be, the play was described as reasonably successful and

acted "with Applause."[27] Genest, in his history of the English stage, described
it as a "very good Farce," and it became part of the repertory, having recorded
performances in 1699, 1703, and 1711, after its initial run.[28]

In order to understand the design and effect of Mary Pix's next comedy, *The
Innocent Mistress* (1697), it is necessary to look briefly at some other plays of the
nineties, as these are the models from which Pix derives her humor. Thomas
Southerne's *The Wives' Excuse* (1691), John Crowne's *The Married Beau* (1694),
Cibber's *Love's Last Shift* (1696), Dryden's *The Husband His Own Cuckold* (1696),
and Vanbrugh's early plays, *The Relapse* (1696) and *The Provoked Wife* (1697),
are all comedies in which the nature of a married relationship tends to dominate
the play. The quality of married life in these versions seems very little if at all
improved over that depicted in Wycherley's *Country Wife* (first performed in
1675). In *Comedy and Society from Congreve to Fielding*, John Loftis points out that
by the end of the century, "playwrights were working with stereotypes, most of
which were already established—and some long established—in the first decade after the Restoration,"[29] and the loveless or boring marriage, whose te-
dium is only relieved by the adultery of either husband or wife, was a staple of
the Restoration repertory. But marital freedom, which in the Restoration court
and on the Restoration stage meant sexual license, in the post-Revolutionary
period (that is, after 1688) was more likely to mean only the freedom to visit
one's friends or to live apart from one's spouse. The moral climate of the times
had changed. Obedience to one's husband, while it could still be legally enforced, was no longer given the same customary sanction. The idea of the companionate marriage seems to have begun to replace old notions of stringent
hierarchy and wifely docility. After 1688, marital obedience was more likely to
mean obedience to the demands of individual conscience or to the moral sua-
sions of middle-class society, at least for those living outside aristocratic
circles.[30] For the playwrights this was a serious constraint upon comic wit,
which for the past thirty-five years had been based upon such perquisites of
male power as hostile sexual jokes, *double entendres*, and comedies of male intrigue, seduction, and adultery.

In the changed atmosphere of England in the 1690s, writing for the theater
was not at all what it had been during the Restoration; the "Merry Monarch,"
Charles II, was dead, and the theater he loved was dead as well—or at least
moribund. John Loftis is just one of the scholars who has pointed out the effects of William III's indifference to the theater. The moralistic attitudes of the
king and queen provided support for critics of the stage and for active reform
groups which were stimulated in the early nineties by the moral climate of the
court, well before the Collier controversy erupted in 1698.[31] Dudley Bahlman,
in *The Moral Revolution of 1688*, describes the rise and growth of the "Societies

for the Reformation of Manners," which began to be active in London before 1692.[32] Audiences were also changing. While recent scholarship has effectively criticized earlier assumptions that the theater up to the end of the seventeenth century drew playgoers almost exclusively from a circle of courtiers and aristocratic wits, it seems equally evident that the 1690s saw an increase in theater attendance by the bourgeoisie.[33]

This new audience seemed to be divided in its expectations. On the one hand, evidence from revivals of older Restoration bawdy comedies indicates that many of them remained popular; but, like the readership for novels that would develop in the next 150 years, audiences as well as preachers wanted plays to reflect their familiar reality and their familiar ethical and social values. The theater might be an amusement, but it was also perceived as an important moral influence, or rather immoral influence, on its audience. This was undoubtedly a reflection of the Puritan revolution of the mid-seventeenth century, as well as part of the ongoing aesthetic debate about the importance of verisimilitude in the arts. In addition to this general change in attitude, Henry Pedicord has identified other kinds of changes that did not help the struggling new playwrights. He refers in particular to the work of John Dennis, the eighteenth-century critic, who "deplored three types of persons" coming into theaters at this time, including those who had little education, such as foreign immigrants (many of them Huguenot), newly rich war profiteers, and a restless class of dispossessed younger sons.[34]

The playwrights of the day were naturally anxious to please these audiences, referred to by Arthur Scouten and Robert Hume as "The Cranky Audiences of 1697–1703,"[35] as despairing prologues and pleading epilogues of the time testify, but they were struggling to represent a rapidly changing social reality that included separation and even divorce (after 1697) as a solution to the problem of unhappy marriages. Women's attitudes and their roles in society were also changing. They were becoming more generally educated and more outspoken about their desire for personal freedom and recognition, while they were also more keenly aware of a moral responsibility toward the family that was not necessarily shared by their husbands and brothers. Solutions for offstage marital and personal problems that would satisfy women's new demands were still in the future; the law courts and the churches were as confused as the individual. It is no wonder that in this moral and social climate playwrights found comedies that pleased, that were moral and were also realistic, very hard to create. The most interesting plays of the nineties reflect this confusion and uncertainty, but those written by men often fail to portray women and women's problems with insight or sympathy.[36]

Southerne's *The Wives' Excuse*, a comedy which both Susan Staves and Robert

Hume admire,[37] is similar in tone and attitude to other plays about marriage produced during the nineties. The opening scene (which runs to almost five pages of dialogue) shows a group of footmen playing hazard while waiting to escort their mistresses home from a concert. Their conversation turns upon the adulterous sex lives of their employers and the way their own incomes are augmented by pimping, accepting bribes for sexual favors, and carrying messages to and from the ladies' lovers. The heroine, Mrs. Friendall, is spoken of pleasantly; all of the other women are attacked. The speech of the third footman is typical: "Every man has hopes of a new marry'd woman, for she marries to like her man. And if upon tryal she finds she can't like her husband, she'll find somebody else that she can like, in a very little time" (I, i, p. 2).[38] Mrs. Witwoud, the least attractive of the women, is acting as guardian to her young cousin, a virgin, who, as Mrs. Witwoud complacently announces, has been carried home "by that rogue, Wilding . . . for when these young wenches once set their hearts upon't, everything gives them an opportunity to ruin themselves" (I, iii, p. 13). She later makes a weak offer to pimp for Wilding if he will leave cousin Fanny's reputation "unsullied." All of the women are present in the play as objects to be seduced rather than as persons; they express no ideas, no attitudes, and no interests that are not sexual. The one exception is Mrs. Friendall, and most of the mental and emotional energy she displays is focused on her husband. The women are incapable of self-awareness or honesty; they are nasty to one another in private and falsely charming in public. Scenes between female characters are few and very brief; two of the four consist entirely of fierce quarrels.

Lovemore, whose charm must rest on his physical beauty since he seems to have nothing else, spends the entire play trying one scheme after another to get Mrs. Friendall into bed, knowing her to be sexually virtuous as well as beautiful. And her only necessary virtue is her chastity, for part of her responsibility as a wife is to tell lies for her husband when he demands it. Lovemore, at the end of the play, is still scheming to seduce her; he is not convinced (none of the men are) that even a "good" woman can hold out forever. Mr. Friendall is unwittingly his best ally, as he is bored by matrimony, detests his wife, and spends all his time chasing other women. Why he doesn't find Mrs. Friendall attractive when everyone else in the play does is never explained. Evidently the fact of their marriage is reason enough (in the best Restoration tradition), as Mr. Friendall boasts that he married her for money, not for love, and to use the cover of matrimony for his own intrigues. Mrs. Friendall's resistance to seduction is based on self-respect, but she is given no active part to play in her own situation except to protect her husband's reputation by her dignity and her lies, and her virtue by passive resistance. A character named Courtall says, "For

Women are by nature well inclined. Our follies frighten 'em from being kind"
(IV, iii, p. 45). In this world, "kind" refers only to sexual generosity. Earlier in
the play Mrs. Witwoud says, "The best commendation of virtue is, that every
Man has a design to put it to the tryal" (II, iii, p. 24).

I have described this play at length because, while it is more unpleasant than
most, it is this collection of stereotypes and hostile jokes to which Mary Pix's
next play, *The Innocent Mistress*, is both reaction and response. Plays like *The
Wives' Excuse* seem to be typical attempts of the decade to modify the Restoration comic model by tacking onto it a virtuous and long-suffering heroine and
a more or less obnoxious husband or lover who is criticized by his more likeable friends for his treatment of his woman (even when all the men behave in
similar ways), and by keeping everyone—more often than not—*out* of the beds
of people they are not married to. The Restoration comedy model, which could
still be lively and funny coming from the pen of a genius such as Congreve, or
which became broadened and transformed by Vanbrugh, had become stale and
repetitive in the hands of less talented imitators. Its most obvious sources
of humor were misogynist jokes and attacks on the morals, talents, and sexual
charms of all the female characters except the heroine. The myths it perpetu-
ated were those of women's uncontrollable sexual appetites, their dishonesty,
their greedy and competitive relationships with other women, and their passiv-
ity and helplessness.

The "new" comedy model, referred to by Robert Hume as "humane" comedy, began to appear more and more often in the nineties; it is described by
Hume as "much more sympathetic. Faults are less harshly judged; . . . writers
are able to acknowledge a basic goodness in individuals. . . . Humane comedy
is much more tolerant, less critical." However, Hume's own analysis of the
plays of Vanbrugh in a later chapter tends to contradict this statement.[39] Susan
Staves asserts that "the comedies and plays of the last decade or so of the
seventeenth century generally insist on the goodness of the heroine. . . .
Most . . . insist on more equal standards of behavior from husband and wife
and idealize marriages where both partners are equally chaste and . . . possessed of equally refined sensibilities." Elsewhere in this same chapter she
says, "The heated misogynist/antimisogynist debate of the earlier seventeenth
century . . . by the end of the century has tipped in favor of the anti-
misogynists."[40] Both of these critics in discussing the male playwrights' comedies of this decade fail to notice the persistence of misogyny in most of these
plays and in the "satyrs," pamphlets, and sermons of the time.[41] As well as
comedies, which retained as staple items the harsh treatment of women, other
contemporary attacks on the sex included such works as "The Playhouse"
(1685) by Robert Gould. The 1689 edition of his poems includes a text of this
work which extends over twenty-four pages, of which about eighteen consist of

attacks on women—as actors, writers, and members of the theater audience—for their "whoring," lewdness, dirtiness, and bad breath. In this same volume Gould includes another poem on the specific immorality of women writers in which he says, "Their verses are as vicious as their tails / Both are exposed alike to public view."[42]

The Innocent Mistress seems to have been written as a humorous defense of women against a wider range of insults than those described above. In addition to the general misogyny of the plays and poems, the decade included more specific attacks on a new kind of woman, the educated woman, on whose behalf Mary Pix was also prepared to speak. In her day, as sometimes in ours, intelligence and learning in the females of the species have been ridiculed. No amount of evidence to the contrary seems to alter the stereotype of beautiful stupidity or that of the ugly and sexless woman with brains. Several attacks on learned women appear on the stage during the early nineties,[43] but the culmination of all the literary hostility was *The Female Wits*, which expanded upon the ideas of earlier comedies to attach the supposed immorality and absurdity of learned women to the three living poets it satirizes. While there are not many known responses to the published poetic satires, the direct response of the three victims to *The Female Wits* is stage history. Delariviere Manley had already withdrawn from Drury Lane as a result of her quarrel with the actors; her play, *The Royal Mischief*, was produced at Lincoln's Inn Fields in April, 1696, and lasted six days—a very good initial run for novice work at this time.[44] But after *The Female Wits* appeared, Manley stayed away from the stage for ten years. Catharine Trotter, who was more gently treated, was not discouraged; she simply took her next play, *The Fatal Friendship*, to Betterton's company, where it appeared in 1698.

Mary Pix also took her next play to Lincoln's Inn Fields, and while it is assumed that she made no other response to the satire, I don't think that that is quite true. For unlike the other novice women, Pix by this time had had two reasonably successful plays produced by the Drury Lane Company: the tragedy, *Ibrahim, 13th Emperor of the Turks*, and the farce, *The Spanish Wives*.[45] By reasonably successful I mean that they had initial runs of at least three days and were part of the repertory for the next several years. Not only was *The Female Wits* an unfair attack on women authors by men who were hiding behind anonymity, but the actors involved included men such as Powell and Cibber who, as novice writers themselves, were competing with the women—and in Powell's case, at least, unsuccessfully. The idea that their wages as actors were in part paid by the audiences drawn to her work must have rankled with Pix, although there is no direct evidence of this. She had every reason, however, to feel that if she continued to write and improve her success, she would be the next to be as harshly treated as Manley or as grossly insulted as Mrs. Barry had been by the satire in "The Playhouse."[46] I think Pix's response to the comedies of the nineties and most particularly to *The Female Wits* was *The Innocent Mistress*, in which she alters for her own purposes the comic conventions used by D'Urfey, Southerne, Cibber, Vanbrugh, and Crowne, and in which, without directly attacking anyone, she gently satirizes their misogynist and cynical plays.

The Innocent Mistress (produced in June, 1697) was suited to the ample resources of the Lincoln's Inn Fields Company, as it demanded a large cast used in a complex multiple plot involving four romancing couples and several marriages. It was described in Jacob's *Poetical Register* as having "met with very good success, though acted in the Summer Season."[47] The lovers in the play include a rakish beau, Sir Francis Wildlove; a sincere young lover, Beaumont, rather like the character of Young Bellair in *The Man of Mode*; Spendall, a man-about-town hoping to snare a rich wife; and the hero, an unhappily married man, Sir Charles Beauclair. Their lady loves include Mrs. Beauclair (Sir Charles's niece), a witty and independent woman attracted to Sir Francis; Arabella, Beaumont's beloved, who is the victim of a plot to control her inheritance; Peggy (Sir Charles's stepdaughter by his wife's first marriage), who is rather like Hoyden in *The Relapse*; and Bellinda, whose virtuous love for the married Sir Charles brings her nothing but misery and occasional chaste conversation with her lover. While these characters all represent familiar types in some ways, their particular behavior and circumstances reverse many of the stock situations used by male playwrights.

Although Pix has as her central plot the story of Sir Charles's and Lady Beauclair's unhappy marriage, she begins by making the husband, rather than the wife, the virtuous and wronged partner of the loveless marriage—the first significant reversal. Pix doesn't suggest that Sir Charles was married against his will, but that he was persuaded to it when he was immature. In this reversal of the more usual situation it is a man, rather than a woman, who was pushed into an injudicious match: " 'Twas a detested match. Ruling friends and cursed avarice joined this unthinking youth to the worst of women" (I, p. 5). He is hardly better off than Lady Brute in *The Provoked Wife*, but is more kindly treated by society for his mistake. His wife, Lady Beauclair, is satirized as an example of a completely uncultured and vulgar person; she is the female equivalent of Sir John Brute in her stupidity, fondness for drink, and lack of grace. She is the opposite of the learned ladies, displaying instead an ignorance which makes her genuinely ridiculous:

> *Sir Charles*: Nay, I have often urged ye to diversions in hopes it would have altered that unquiet mind, but all in vain.

> *Lady Beauclair*: Divartions! What divartions: Yes, you had me to the play-house, and the first thing I saw was an ugly, black devil kill his wife for nothing, then your Metridate, King o' the Potecaries, your Timon the Athiest, the Man in the Moon, and all the rest. Nonsense! Stuff! I hate em!
>
> (III, p. 24).

She makes a fine burlesque of literary criticism; nor is she more modest or less vulgar for her lack of learning and understanding.

Later Lady Beauclair attempts to market her daughter as if she were a madam and the daughter a piece of sexual merchandise:

> *Lady Beauclair*: Lord, Peggy, you're too forward! I wonder on ye now. Sir, she is my daughter, and she'll be worth eight thousand pounds, and a better penny. I would not have her cast away, Sir.
> *Lyewell* [a lawyer]: To be thrown into a young gentleman's arms with a great estate will be a good cast, I take it, Madam.
> *Lady Beauclair*: If I were satisfied in that!
>
> (IV, p. 37)

Unlike Southerne's Mrs. Witwoud, she is marketing her daughter into marriage, not prostitution; the parallel is, however, unavoidably suggestive. Lady Beauclair's ability to drive a shrewd bargain is impaired by her ignorance. She completely misses the ambiguity in the lawyer's remark, nor can she read or understand the marriage contract she has negotiated for Peggy; it is in Latin: " 'Noverint etcetera . . . ' No, sir, I don't understand law. But you look like a good, honest man, Sir, and I dare take your word" (IV, p. 37). While these scenes would be obviously amusing to an audience, they also have the effect of exposing—and indeed reversing—the fatuous argument of other plays that a lack of learning and a limited experience of the world make women somehow more moral and attractive.

In contrast to Lady Beauclair and Peggy, the other women in the play are witty, intelligent, and independent, without sacrificing their virtue, their moral understanding, or their ability to attract men. Sir Charles is the beloved of a woman whose passion for him arose before she knew he was married, and whose love and virtuous constancy are presented to us as the result of her fondness for reading:

> *Bellinda*: In vain I fly to books, the tuneful numbers give me not a moment's ease. . . . Here, sweet bard, thou suits me well, "My anxious hours roll heavily away, / Deprived of sleep by night or peace by day."
>
> (I, p. 4)

> Had my glass but been my idol, my mind loose, unconstant, wavering, like my sex, then I might have 'scaped these pangs.
>
> (IV, p. 39)

Bellinda is in hiding from a forced marriage to a man whose virtues were not those of her favorite romances. Here is another reversal, a new twist on the comic pattern of young men who flee abroad under assumed names when pursued by debt or crimes, or young women who retire into the country when they are disappointed in love or have disobeyed their parents. Bellinda has fled to the center of London and is living independently under an assumed name to avoid marriage to a man who probably had never read a novel in his life. Although the passion she has for reading has caused her present suffering, we are told that it has also furnished her with harmless occupation for idle hours (London for a virtuous woman seems in this instance far more boring than the depths of Shropshire). These romances evidently provide the source for Bellinda's speeches which seem derived equally from Mlle. Scudéry and the bombast of romantic tragedy: "See him no more, him whom I could not live a day, an hour without! No more behold his eyeballs tremble with respectful passion! Hear no more the soft falling accents of his charming tongue! View him dying at my feet no more! . . . Racks, gibbets and dungeons, can they equal losing all my soul admires?" (IV, p. 39). To complete the parodic nature of the character, the role of Bellinda was taken by Elizabeth Barry, the leading tragic actress of her day, popularly assumed to be notoriously promiscuous,[48] and in this comedy playing—at the age of thirty-nine—a never-married woman, acutely conscious of her virtue: " . . . our love is to the modern age unpractised and unknown, yet so strict and so severe are rigid honour's laws, that though not grossly, yet we still offend. . . . full of innocent delight I blushed, and fondly thought this man my amorous stars, in kindness, destined for my happiness, but oh! . . . I that thought to have stood the fairest pattern of my sex, and would have blotted all the annals of guilty love, yet now am lost" (I, p. 5). Since Bellinda has not so far committed—nor indeed does she ever commit— an immoral act, Pix is also playing on the new demand for moral comedy, one which she mentions with some frequency (and occasionally, exasperation) in her prologues and dedications.

The characters of Beaumont, Bellinda, and Peggy are a reversal of the standard Restoration comedy idea that country living necessarily produced vulgarity, ignorance, dullness, and the coarser forms of vice. Mary Pix is one of the first writers of comedy to promote country life as both beneficial and attractive. Peggy, unlike Vanbrugh's Hoyden whom she resembles, is an entirely urban product, while Beaumont and Bellinda, virtuous, cultured, and used to elegance, have entered the city from the country with these qualities. They are neither deluded nor seduced by the kind of life in the city that so enchants Loveless in *The Relapse*. Indeed, Bellinda meets Sir Charles when he rescues her from a mugging. Beaumont is frantic over the covetous greed of Lady Beauclair's brother Cheatall, the city financier who is holding his beloved Arabella hostage, and he thinks of Bellinda as exposed to dangerous temptations because she now lives in London. Pix explored the relative virtues of city and country life in several other comedies even more specifically than in this one. It was a moral reexamination that began in the nineties, reflected both in prose essays and in such later comedies as those of Farquhar and Mary Davys.

As the unhappy spouse in love with another, Sir Charles is not the libertine husband of *Love's Last Shift* or *The Married Beau*, nor is he the male equivalent of Mrs. Friendall. His virtue is comic because it is so unusual and is enforced, not attacked, by the person he loves. His gender works a reversal on the idea of the virtuous and unhappy wife who is victimized by both her lover and her society. His friends support him compassionately; only his wretched wife complains about the denial of her conjugal rights: "Oh the villain, the rogue! . . . Always at home he's sick or his head aches, and he must lie alone" (II, p. 16). (I have found no other examples of it in these early plays, but the headache joke seems to be older than has been generally realized.) In another reversal of the customary, what charms Sir Charles about Bellinda is her mind and character, rather than her seductive beauty or her money: "Though the bauble, gaudy beauty, die, yet sense and humour still remain. On that I should have doted" (V, p. 40).

Sir Francis Wildlove, the rakish character, is also changed by Pix from the Restoration stereotype to suit her purposes. He renounces the rake's usual system of values by insisting that Mrs. Beauclair's fortune, twelve thousand pounds, does not attract him: "Chains of gold won't tempt my freedom from me" (I, p. 3), he says, instead of drinking to get up the courage to either seduce her or propose to her because of her great fortune as so many Restoration rakes have done. Wildlove makes no serious attempts on Mrs. Beauclair's virtue (as she is his friend's niece), but instead is kept from immoral conduct by her trickery. Instead of the seductive rake and helpless virgin or courtesan of other comedies, Mary Pix gives us the helpless rake. Her clever virgin, played by Anne Bracegirdle, the leading comic actress of the time, is the one who in male disguise "seduces" the loose woman whom Wildlove is pursuing. Nor does Mrs. Beauclair preach to him about the way he ought to live or about sexual restraint; instead she confesses to finding his "hearty hug" appealing (II, p. 18). Wildlove does not share the traditional misogyny of rakes and men-about-town any more than he shares their avarice, for he is able to tell good women from bad; he says of Lady Beauclair that she "has neither sense, beauty or good manners" (I, p. 2), and yet, "her carriage is not a satire on the whole sex. It but sets off better wives" (III, p. 24). Like Valentine in Congreve's *Love for Love*, when Wildlove does fall in love he is increasingly serious about it, long before he can persuade his beloved to take his passion seriously. She not only tricks him more than once, but also laughs at him for his inconstancy and easy virtue. He insists that he does not love where he flirts (again an alteration of the Restoration stereotype who denies love altogether), but rather: "Think ye so meanly of me, my heart bestowed among your Sex's shame! No, Madam, Glorious Virtue alone can reach at that. My loving is a diversion I can soon shake off" (IV, p. 31). Unlike his counterparts of an earlier generation, Wildlove has more than persistence and seductiveness to recommend him to Mrs. Beauclair. Pix creates scenes in which we can see his appreciation of her wit and his distaste for the false jilt he is pursuing for mere "diversion." He finally begins to pursue Mrs. Beauclair, and his attraction turns to love when he hears—falsely—that she is married to another. Mrs. Beauclair professes to disbelieve his avowals until he falls "into the romantic style" (IV, p. 46), as she says, and persuades her into matrimony.

The minor romances of Peggy and Arabella are also concluded by marriages, but of rather different kinds. Arabella's lover was chosen before the play opened; only her need to escape from her false guardian delays her happiness. With the aid of an audacious plan, concocted by the clever female servant, Eugenia, Arabella flees from Cheatall, Lady Beauclair's avaricious but stupid brother, to take refuge with Mrs. Beauclair. Cheatall, like Congreve's Foresight in *Love for Love*, is a slave to predictions, but of crystal ball gazers rather than astrologers. Like Macbeth, he is urged on to wicked deeds by a more daring woman, in this case his sister. And like many another older man in more typical comedies, he lusts vainly after a young beauty. When Arabella escapes, Cheatall is persuaded that without his own knowledge he has murdered and dismembered her. The maid has tricked him by pouring red ink all over the bedroom and telling him it is blood. Without remembering the crime, he does remember that his hanging was foretold. He alternates between rage and panic in a funny scene in which his sister tries vainly to assure him that wealth and rank in society place him above the law, and that with Arabella's supposed death he has gained more than he has risked. For the genuine aristocrat of the reign of Charles II, such immunity seems to have been a historical fact, but for the newly rich citizen in an age of reform her assurances are vain and Cheatall knows it: only financial crimes go unpunished in this age.

In the other subplot, Peggy and her new husband, Spendall, are mutually deceived in their expectations of wealth. Spendall has no money of his own, but has cadged dinners and gifts from Sir Charles; Peggy's marriage settlement disappears into thin air when her father suddenly reappears alive. But Peggy, in another reversal of convention, is not very concerned. She likes marriage and wants adult freedom more than just sex or money. It does not occur to her that she is not loved for herself alone and that she is in danger of being abused by her disappointed husband. Spendall's anger is clear to the audience, however, as if to reinforce Pix's earlier arguments that ignorance for women is anything but bliss. The other women in the play rally around Peggy, expecting to befriend her and educate her once she is detached from Lady Beauclair's influence. One is led to assume that Sir Charles will keep a kind of moral eye on Spendall, especially if Peggy's rediscovered father can be induced to grant her a dowry.

The women in the play represent a wide range of types: the witty heroine, the imprisoned heiress, the educated lady, the untutored raw girl, the vulgar older wife, the clever lady's maid, the kept woman. All but the kept woman, Jenny Flywife, end up with appropriate marriage partners, and even she is not scorned but treated with a certain sympathy. Mrs. Beauclair gives her a present because Jenny was the woman who unwittingly assisted her in the trick she played against Wildlove. Throughout the play, these women have encouraged one another with their problems of the heart and they have their reward.

Mary Pix's main plot is resolved with the discovery that Sir Charles's and Lady Beauclair's marriage is bigamous, and with Sir Charles's revelation that he has never slept with his "wife." Her first husband has turned up in London, very much alive and keeping his mistress in the house next door to the respectable Bellinda. The long-suffering hero does not need a divorce or separate maintenance; as in Pix's earlier farce, the unhappy marriage is no marriage at all. Lady Beauclair's punishment for her previous unkind and crude behavior is to return to her first husband and to know that the "rich" marriage into which she pushed her daughter was a fraud. Bellinda (now using her real name, Marianne) and Sir Charles are united in passionate transports of bliss. Beaumont and Arabella and probably even Sir Francis Wildlove and Mrs. Beauclair seem destined to live happily ever after. All three romantic couples are well matched in a comic world that both repeats and reverses theatrical conventions. In the final reversals of the play, Cheatall is enormously relieved and contrite when Arabella turns up alive; his experience causes him to renounce his sister as an influence in his life and become a friend to the others. While the bridegrooms of this play are the rapturous believers in the joys of matrimony that tradition tells us women are supposed to be, it is Cheatall who cynically warns the company about the inevitable aftermath of marriage when he says, "But hear me, ladies, 'faith all young, handsome fellows talk just so before matrimony. Seven years hence let me hear of pantings, heavings and raptures. No, gadzooks, scarce risings then" (V, p. 52). And of all this company it is Mrs. Beauclair who thanks him for his realistic reminder.

Much comedy of this period has been dismissively described as reformist or sentimental, yet Mary Pix's alterations to the comic norm are a kind of rational burlesque of contemporary plays. Rather than didactic or naively romantic, her resolution scene seems appropriate for a woman writing about women. Marriage for the unmarried is necessary, and yet can be seen realistically rather than cynically, if the terms are right for both partners. But the comic convention that uses marriage as closure is not useful to a plot that begins with marriage. For a woman in the seventeenth century, the separation that resolves such dark comedies as *The Married Beau*, *The Provoked Wife*, or, later, *The Beaux' Stratagem*, had nothing comic about it. In the real as well as the stage world, her life was closed by a situation that did not offer her a chance to marry again or even to love again without shame. Only the fantasy that no true marriage had taken place would do.

I have lingered over the details of *The Innocent Mistress* because its text suggests the deliberate rearrangement of both old and new comic devices for purposes unique in this decade to its female creator. Mary Pix did not go unrewarded for her skill. Not only was the play a success, but her accomplishment (or her response to *The Female Wits*) seems to have prompted George Powell, as an actor-manager at Drury Lane, to steal her next play while pretending to reject it as a vehicle for the Patent Company.[49] Pix was, in my opinion, both revenging herself on the Drury Lane Company and establishing a career as a playwright with *The Innocent Mistress*. In the process she embarked upon a theatrical partnership that would enable her to survive the problems of male criticism and the competition for production opportunities, problems that her female contemporaries were unable to overcome successfully. This is not the place in which to give a detailed history of that partnership, that is, the cooperation which I believe existed between Pix and Elizabeth Barry; however, I am sure that the characterizations and language of much of *The Innocent Mistress* derive from that association. There is some evidence that she was aided by Congreve in her fight with Powell over plagiarism and we know that all the rest of her plays were produced at Lincoln's Inn Fields, but the debt she must have owed to Barry is not recorded anywhere.[50] It is suggested, however, in the types of plays and roles Pix wrote from this time on. While her obvious gift was for comedy, half of her plays were tragedies with starring roles for Elizabeth Barry. And the comedies she did write were not about young virgins or ingenue maidens, but were vehicles about widows for an actress entering her forties. Barry, although not primarily a comic actress at all, had a principal role in almost every one. As a Lincoln's Inn Fields shareholder, Barry's power to sponsor plays gave Mary Pix an opportunity to say things about women—their characters, their lives, their morals, and their feelings—that the male playwrights of the period either did not believe or were not interested in saying.

Some of the ideas about women that Pix expressed in her first two comedies appear again in her later plays, particularly in *The Beau Defeated* and *The Different Widows*, plays in which she describes women who learn from other women how best to arrange their lives and their prospects of marriage. *The Beau Defeated* (1700) is, as Mary Pix said in her dedication, partially translated from

Dancourt's *Le Chevalier à la Mode*, written in 1687.[51] But the changes and additions Pix chose to make in both character and plot reveal her comic gifts and her dramatic and moral concerns, and make her play much more than an adaptation. Dancourt's version has as its central characters a titled beau looking for a rich wife, a middle-class widow trying to move into upper-class life by marrying the beau, and her niece, who thinks the flirtatious Chevalier has honorable intentions toward her. There is also a clever maid, who is the widow's confidante; a Baroness, representing the old aristocracy, who wants the Chevalier for herself and whose hobby is litigation; her lawyer, who wants to marry the widow; and the widow's brother-in-law, who disapproves of her social pretensions. The Chevalier makes love to both the widow and the niece, of whose relationship he is unaware. Because they are kin, they accidentally discover his duplicity, and as long as the other woman does not win him by default, they are both eager to reject him. Madame Patin—the widow—marries the lawyer after all; her niece—Lucile—accepts the lawyer's son, whom her father had earlier chosen for her. In accepting him she says, "In my present state of grief [having discovered the Chevalier's deceit], my father, I will do all that you wish" (V, p. 92), a submissive speech that has no parallel in Mary Pix's revision.

The opening scene of *The Beau Defeated* is a literal translation from Dancourt, moving from the pushy French *arriviste* in Paris to the newly wealthy city widow in London. As in the Dancourt play it is a conversation between the clever maid and the widow about class, the pretension to it, and the vulgar display of wealth. Pix used the clever female servant (rather than the clever manservant) in other plays as well; this scene suited her style:

> *Betty*: What's the matter, Madam? What has happend to you?
> *Mrs. Rich*: An affront . . . Ah! I die; an affront! . . . I faint; I cannot speak. A chair quickly.
> *Betty*: (giving a chair) An affront! To you, Madam, an affront! Is it possible!
> *Mrs. Rich*: [The Duchess] with a scornful smile, cried, "Hold thy peace, Citizen!" Struck me quite dumb.
> *Betty*: Citizen! Citizen! To a lady in a gilt coach, lined with crimson velvet, and hung round with a gold fringe!
>
> (I, p. 1)

But Pix adds a second plot, with a leading role for Anne Bracegirdle and a romantic hero to win her. It is the relation between these two plots, as well as changes in point of view and emphasis, that sets *The Beau Defeated* apart from its source. The Bracegirdle role is that of a second widow, Lady Landsworth, who has come to London to enjoy herself and spend her inheritance. After enduring a loveless marriage to an older man, Lady Landsworth now has freedom, money, and property and can look about her for a more satisfactory mate. She represents country virtue, rather as Bellinda does in *The Innocent Mistress*, instead of country coarseness. Her rational character provides a contrast to the city widow's affectation and vulgarity. Lady Landsworth's search for a second husband is, as Nancy Cotton describes it, for "a man virtuous and witty; he must also be poor and unaware that she is rich."[52] It is a piece of deliberate comic irony that she finds Young Clerimont at the playhouse when she is masked. Lady Landsworth is not the kind of loose woman whom the moralists criticized for attending the playhouse in a vizard. She also contradicts in her character the then-current assumptions about the insatiable lusts of the sexually experienced woman by refusing to fall into the arms of a witty and attractive man until she has satisfied herself of his sincerity. Naturally, given the theater as a setting for their first meeting, each of the characters thinks the other one to be promiscuous, but when the confusions of the plot are resolved, she has an attractive younger son for her new husband and she has him on her own terms. Their relationship is tested in the course of the action by their attempts to define sexual honesty and to establish virtue as a basis for their love. This is contrasted to the plot in which Mrs. Rich, the widow, is willing to settle for appearance and what passes with her for reputation.

The main plot, altered from Dancourt, is both comically and morally controlled by the question of whether appearance is truth and to what degree. Mrs. Rich is foolishly unable to distinguish between quality and its surface, as she parades around London in her gilded coach and is gulled by Lady Basset (the Baroness character) into gaming and entertaining a group of social parasites. Lady Basset resolves to trick the widow, to punish her for social pretension and take her money. To this end she introduces Mrs. Rich to a "beau," who in Pix's play is an alcoholic servant in disguise, but Mrs. Rich is so blinded by the false title of "Sir John Roverhead" and so irritated by her brother-in-law's attempts to guide her behavior that she has no ability to see behind the facade of her new life. Unlike Lady Landsworth, she cannot apply moral tests to the man of her choice, for she is choosing the appearance rather than the person. At the end of the play, when "Sir John" is unmasked as a footman and Lady Basset as a sharper, Mrs. Rich has married the elder Clerimont, the brother of Lady Landsworth's lover. Although Mrs. Rich is motivated in her marriage by a desire for revenge—when Sir John seems to be interested in another woman—she is also tricked into the match by those who genuinely desire her welfare. Her shock at discovering that Clerimont is really a country bumpkin rather than a fashionable gentleman is amended after Lady Landsworth says, "Be reconciled to your new spouse, who is of a noble family, and I promise to introduce ye to persons of merit and honour" (V, p. 46). Lady Landsworth knows that Clerimont is a country squire of limited but genuine qualities, who only needs the widow's money to restore his decayed title and estates. The squire will—one hopes— prove to be as educable as his new wife under the affectionate supervision of their superior friends and connections.

The friendly alliance that Pix creates among her moral female characters has no counterpart in Dancourt's play; its purpose seems to be to educate the other women in this group into honesty, self-awareness, modesty, and common sense. Lucinda, Mrs. Rich's niece, does not marry to please her father (as her original does in Dancourt's version), but at the play's end she is instead to receive an education. Mr. Rich has come to realize how much she needs it, and her aunt's new life and new connections promise an opportunity for her that she, like Peggy in *The Innocent Mistress* or Vanbrugh's Hoyden, has never had. Mrs. Clerimont, the sister of the elder and younger Clerimont, is a woman of sense and quality whose presence in this cast has no equivalent in the French original. She acts as a foil to Mrs. Rich. An urban woman of good character, she is also a friend to Lady Landsworth and a kind of informative chorus for the audience, telling us that her younger brother is, in spite of appearances, a decent young man worth his lady's love. She contracts a sensible marriage to young Belvoir, a friend of her brother approved of by Lady Landsworth. The function of this character and of her relatively trivial romance seems to be twofold. She serves as another moral woman, showing that an ethical life is possible, even in the city, if it is sensibly chosen; she is also a model of the woman who makes an appropriate marriage choice for herself.

It is Lady Landsworth's friendship to Mrs. Rich, in spite of that Lady's appearance of improper living, which helps the merchant's widow to a good second marriage. Lady Landsworth welcomes her as a new sister, saying, "We shall all be fond of ye, for of yourself you are charming and sensible" (V, p. 46). Even if this was not originally true of Mrs. Rich, Lady Landsworth and Mrs. Clerimont make it true. The implication is that Mrs. Rich has never learned how to form her judgments and her friendships, that this is not a permanent defect of character but a flaw in her education which can be amended by her more sensible friends. Even the hostility Mrs. Rich displays toward her niece, an emotion also present in the Dancourt play, is changed in Mary Pix's version. Rather than simply an example of stereotypic competition between women so common in other plays, Mrs. Rich's hostility is part of her ignorance and part of her struggle to move out of her own and her late husband's social class. To educate and help her niece, rather than vilify her, is one of the lessons she learns.

In the second plot, the courtship of Young Clerimont and Lady Landsworth, it is partly the testimony of his landlady, Mrs. Fidget, that helps persuade his beloved that his honesty is greater than it at first appears. Mrs. Fidget, described at the beginning of the action as a kind of procuress and keeper of a questionable rooming house, is persuaded initially by a man to misrepresent her young lodger of whom she is really fond. She is later persuaded by Mrs. Clerimont that honesty will serve the cause of true love better than deceit and in her final appearance in the play emerges as both more moral and more likeable than she was.

In the opening scene, Betty's comments upon the widow's attitude to her relations underline Mrs. Rich's poor sense of her appropriate place in society:

> *Mrs. Rich*: I am resolved and I will be a countess; . . . I'll absolutely break all commerce with those little cits by whose alliance I am debased. . . .
> *Betty*: Mr. Rich, madam, your brother-in-law?
> *Mrs. Rich*: . . . Prithee know better!
> *Betty*: Pardon me, madam, I thought he had been your brother-in-law because he was brother to your deceased husband.
> *Mrs. Rich*: . . . but my husband being dead, fool, Mr. Rich is now no more kin to me than my footman. . . . Nay, even the little minx, his daughter, when we go in my coach together, places herself at the end, by my side.
> *Betty*: Little ridiculous creature!
>
> (I, pp. 2–3)

From the earliest dialogue of the scene the satirical intent of Betty's comment is clearly meant for the "ridiculous" widow, who is indeed very nearly married to a footman after all. When Mrs. Rich is finally reconciled to her brother-in-law it is as part of her education into her proper place in the world. In Mr. Rich Mary Pix has created a man who is probably one of the first attractive middle-class characters in drama. His unaffected manners and non-satiric portrait serve two purposes for Pix: he provides a foil for the humorous character of his sister-in-law; and Mrs. Rich's and his own daughter's inability to learn from a good, if limited, man, emphasizes the roles of the women as necessary moral and social guides for other women. In his concern for the dignity of his own extended family, Mr. Rich conspires with Betty fairly early in the play to trick his sister-in-law into a sensible second marriage; Betty volunteers for the task out of a concern and friendship unique to the work of women writers, whose male peers saw only competition and hostility as typical of a woman's world. Indeed, "Speak not you sir, for I yield only to the ladies" (V, p. 41), a speech addressed to her brother-in-law, could well be taken for Mrs. Rich's motto.

Lady Landsworth not only teaches Mrs. Rich; she also exposes the falseness of Lady Basset and condemns her for her avarice and for taking advantage of another woman. Yet Lady Landsworth herself is far from being a stuffy or didactic character. None of the characters in this play indulge in the heavy-handed moralizing which Cibber and Vanbrugh put in Amanda's mouth in their earlier reform comedies, for example. Lady Landsworth uses trickery and disguise in her affair with Young Clerimont, and has amusing scenes with him while they work out their relationship; she is romp as well as teacher. The scenes derived from Dancourt's play, including Mrs. Rich's struggle to turn herself into a lady of quality, are also highly comic. And by making "Sir John Roverhead" a drunken footman in disguise instead of a genuine aristocrat, Pix has added elements of burlesque and parody. Mrs. Rich's maid, Betty, acts constantly as a chorus, whose asides to the audience make it clear that Mrs. Rich is not an example to follow but an object of ridicule: "Tho' my mistress is fled to Covent Garden, she is as much despised by the real quality, as she is cajoled by the pretenders to it" (I, p. 4). While Dancourt's play has limited social satire as its point and the pretentious widow as its butt, the purpose of the main plot in Pix's comedy is Mrs. Rich's education by another woman into a proper set of values, an education which is implicitly not available in London society. Nor is Mrs. Rich simply an object of derision; her treatment is both comic and sympathetic, a kind of characterization that no male playwright of the period would be likely to consider for this type of older woman.

If the years between 1698 and 1702 represented the peak of the reformist attack upon the stage, it is suggested by Bahlman's study of moral reform that the tide began to recede soon after.[53] It is also likely that in these years of maximum competition between the two theater companies, as Judith Milhous points out, the hunger for audiences was greater than ever.[54] Other evidence of the effect of this quest for an audience may perhaps be inferred from the incomplete production information from this period. Both the reformist attack and the competition for audiences weighed heavily on Mary Pix. In spite of her preference for and skill in comedy, she turned out four tragedies between the autumn of 1698 and the summer of 1701; *The Beau Defeated* was her only comedy script during this time. As *A Comparison between the Two Stages* points out, "the Town, not being able to furnish out two good audiences every day, changed their inclinations for the two houses, as they found themselves inclined to comedy or tragedy. If they desired a tragedy, they went to Lincolns-Inn-fields; if . . . comedy, they flocked to Drury-Lane, which was the reason that several days but one house acted. But by this variety of humour in the Town, they shared pretty equally the profit."[55] This decision for tragedy would suit Betterton and Barry, but a writer tied to one house as Pix was had then little choice in the matter of genre. Milhous suggests in her discussion of the competition that a policy of mutual toleration replaced cutthroat competition between the death of King William in 1702 and the opening of the new Queen's Theatre in the Haymarket in April, 1705.[56] The relaxation of competition and the perhaps easier moral climate of the first years of Queen Anne's reign seem to have changed theatrical production opportunities for Mary Pix, as her next play indicates.

With her next comedy, *The Different Widows* (1703), Pix returned to a broader comedy of intrigue and to sexually looser conventions than she had used in earlier plays. In her prologue she acknowledges the altered taste of the times, but laments the loss of wit:

> Morn, after Morn, I've sought, yet could not get
> (If Life had layn at Stake) one Drachm of Wit;
> You'd swear I'd gone a Begging in the Pit.
> . . . .
> . . . to Will's I took my round,
> But not one Poet there was to be found,
> Except the Author of the *Country Wife*,
> But faith, I durst not Wake him for my Life:
> Lest his Plain Dealing *Muse* should let you hear
> Such Stinging Truths you'd not know how to bear
> And make you (in a Pet) our House forswear.

In this play she repeated an earlier plot device by contrasting two widows' lives and values, while intensifying her earlier social criticisms. Lady Bellmont represents rational virtue and the sensible elegance of country life; her sister, Lady Gaylove, personifies urban vulgarity and vice—disguised under the socially acceptable veneer of reputation. As a fashionable woman, Lady Gaylove pretends to be much younger than she really is. Her adult children, Marina and Squire Gaylove, are dressed as children, kept in the nursery, and deprived of education. The principal romance of the comedy is between Lady Bellmont's rakish son, Sir James, and her wealthy friend, Angelica, whose values are also those of the well-bred country gentry. Angelica designs to reform Sir James and persuade him to marry: "He says, I hear, no Woman ever Conquered or outwitted him; now I fancy I have as many crotchets in my head as he, and I am sure I have more money, and so have most likelihood not to fail in my design" (II, p. 13). Valentine, a friend of Angelica and Sir James's cousin, abducts Lady Gaylove's sequestered offspring because he feels sorry for them and is very attracted to Marina. Lady Bellmont agrees to take her niece under her protection and educate her, while Valentine attempts to turn the young squire into a gentleman.

There are several minor plots revolving around the group of people who frequent Lady Gaylove's house. These involve two city couples of different social class, several beaux, and much sexual intrigue and flirtation. No liaisons are consummated although there is much tumbling into closets and under beds, and there are numerous narrow escapes, discoveries, and comically missed opportunities. Most of the satiric targets in these scenes are similar to those Pix used in earlier plays. They include the social aspirations of the newly rich Sir Antony Loveman and his wife; the quarrelsome dissenting merchant, Drawl, whose wife yearns for fashionable life and lovers; the beau and fop, Dandle and Careless, who have more affectation than style, and who live by flattery and parasitic friendships with the well-to-do. The subplots also include the kept woman, Lady Courtall, who uses her lover for economic security but is not in love with him and does not really like sex; Lord Courtall, who treats his common-law wife as if she were bought property (which she is) while he pursues Lady Loveman; and finally Lady Gaylove herself, a widow who makes money by pimping for both men and women, by concealing lovers at her house and offering it for assignations, and probably by blackmailing her acquaintances. She is constantly and hypocritically concerned for her reputation (her "decorums" as she calls it) and so must be continually bribed to do favors for her "dearest friends." Sir James Bellmont visits her house because it is a good place to meet women, and his mother and Angelica visit Lady Gaylove to criticize her way of life.

The friendship between Angelica and Lady Bellmont is used by Pix as a device for moral conversations. Two of these are particularly important as they represent consistent attitudes throughout Pix's work. The first occurs in the second act. While Squire Gaylove wanders about acting and speaking like a complete dolt, Angelica speaks to her friend about the importance of education, and Lady Bellmont suggests that natural folly is probably better or at least less dreadful than sophisticated wickedness. The girl, Marina, wants an education, as she is woefully aware of her lack of accomplishment, and goes gratefully to her aunt for help. She does learn and acquires grace and elegance as well as judgment; Valentine is pleased with her improvement, falls in love with her, and marries her. Marina's brother, on the other hand, has no innate yearning for self-development, but wants adult status and privileges such as a carriage, a sword, and fine clothes. Squire Gaylove, in spite of Valentine's efforts, is virtually ineducable and remains a boor with a fop's exterior, rather than a gentleman. One of the funniest scenes in the play is the one in which he is being fitted out as a man of fashion. He attempts to learn to take snuff, trips over his new sword, and almost suffocates in a cloud of powder from his new wig (IV, pp. 36–37). The conversation between the two friends emphasizes the difference between the young man and the young lady and directs the audience's attention to the distinction.

The other conversation Lady Bellmont has with Angelica is about her sister's way of life and her son's libertine habits. Lady Bellmont suggests that "those poor creatures [men] can't help it, and she [Lady Gaylove] can" (II, p. 12). Her statement is one of the earliest assertions in literature that men are morally weaker than women, and because of male lust, rather than female trickery, have poorer control over their impulses than women. Male playwrights thought differently. Even as recently as *The Relapse* (1696), Vanbrugh had placed heavy emphasis on the active role of the seductress Berinthia in Loveless's fall from virtue. Mary Pix is again reversing male myths of the time about the incurable ignorance, vanity, and sexual appetites of women. She is not unique in her attempts to change the stereotype of woman-as-depraved-temptress. Many women writing plays, essays, novels, poems, and journalism during this post-Restoration era were joined in the effort to alter contemporary attitudes.[57] Mary Pix's difference from most others engaged in this struggle is that her virtuous heroines are not boring.

Angelica's role of reforming woman in the play is funny rather than "sentimental." She catechizes Sir James about his notions of love and ridicules his argument for instinct as a justification for his behavior; he likens himself to the "happy Animals" while Angelica suggests instead, "Then you imitate the Brutes?" (II, p. 23). She is responsive to his suggestion that reason makes a difference; she is no prude and is evidently attracted by both his person and his arguments, but manages to escape his pursuit by various tricks and disguises, including a pretense that she is his natural sister. Sir James suspiciously responds, "If not my sister, then fair Sorceress, beware!" (II, p. 25), while she escapes from him without telling him her true name or rank in society. Angelica's final trick on her libertine lover is to agree to sleep with him, when he says, "I am so furiously in Love, I believe I will grow constant and change no more" (IV, p. 44). But he must marry her first. She offers to release him after one day if they don't suit one another; he hesitates, then agrees. Before the marriage can be consummated, however, she has him arrested for unpaid debts and thrown in prison.

Sir James is at first like Dorimant in prefering wenching to wiving. When his cousin Valentine proposes the idea of matrimony to him he replies, "Won't a dose of Opium do as well?" (III, p. 26). But none of his attempts on women during the course of the play succeed. Angelica, by pretending to be his wife in one scene, interrupts a liaison with Lady Courtall, who to her credit (and following Pix's usual pattern of women who help women) leaves Sir James alone when she thinks him married. Other attempts of his are interrupted by various jealous husbands. The result for him is a kind of exasperated weariness with the futility of illicit love: "If this be variety, I shall grow sick on it and rather choose to be confined to one, than thus to be tantalized by the whole sex" (III, pp. 34–35). He has, however, only a temporary inclination toward virtue, which disappears when Lady Loveman approaches him. She herself hesitates, wishing to be, she says, "both gay and innocent" (III, p. 35). Sir James suggests that this is deceitful on her part, but while they are still negotiating, Angelica sends for him and he leaves Lady Loveman, who concludes that she may as well remain faithful to her husband since men are so fickle. Both men and women of fashion in this corrupt world are shown to be opportunists whose morals are expedient and temporary and whose way of life fails to promote any degree of personal happiness. Only Sir James is sufficiently self-aware to question his own behavior.

All the deceivers and hypocrites in Lady Gaylove's circle are exposed in the course of the action and most of them, rather than being sentimentally reformed, are punished. What keeps Sir James from being fully a member of this morally corrupt group is his honesty. He chases women, but he is no hypocrite, he will not pretend to be other than he is. Angelica sees this virtue in him and attempts to cure him of his wenching by teasing him, while Sir James's mother, just like a mother, tries to cure him by scolding. But to no avail. Sir James is not led astray by dreadful females, but admits his own responsibility for the games of love and chance he plays. As Pix's reference to Wycherley in the prologue suggests, she is reminding her audience of *The Plain Dealer*, only her "plain dealer" is more likeable and less angry at the world than Manly, and, as his plain dealing doesn't make him less inclined to chase women, more believable. Even Sir James's attempts on other women are made according to his and their desire for intrigue, for he believes, "A woman's never to be ravished against her will" (III, p. 34). His growing awareness of his own feelings and the failures in his seduction attempts make his reform gradually, but genuinely, probable. Like Wildlove in Pix's earlier comedy, Sir James becomes exasperated with a life of conquest that, thanks to Angelica, leads finally to frustration rather than sexual satisfaction.

The other characters in the circle of immorality and infidelity fare less well. The merchant Drawl, who has been so suspicious of his wife that he has even dressed as a perfume seller to catch her in an act of betrayal, calls his woman's dress "the outside of Profaneness" (I, p. 8), then uses his disguise to attempt seduction of Lady Gaylove's maid. The women conspire to expose him to his wife, who comes out of hiding and snarls at him, "Thy hypocritical saintship . . . thou false Apostle, thou greater pretender and little performer in everything!" (IV, p. 44). She has, of course, been less than honest herself in pretending to be falsely accused; she has been having an intrigue of her own with the fop, Careless. Drawl acknowledges their mutual dissatisfactions: "Yes, each knowing the other's infirmities, we will go home, and live like the rest of the married world, upbraiding one another" (IV, p. 44). As they are both morally flawed, they are condemned to live together unhappily. The fops, Dandle and Careless, become involved in fake marriages that turn out to be permanent traps. Dandle, thinking he has married Lady Gaylove for her money, turns out to be married to the maid, Lucy. Careless succeeds in tricking Lady Gaylove herself—who did not want to marry at all—into matrimony and ends up with her money, but in having to take her person as well is probably getting a poor bargain. Lady Courtall, after pretending to value a relationship that was only a source of income to her, loses her keeper when she is discovered attempting to take another lover. She sarcastically admits to her dishonesty: "Yes, yes. I ride in his coach, spend his estates . . . love him, oh, mightily!" (IV, p. 42).

Unlike the others, Sir Antony Loveman and his wife are reconciled by her apologies for deceit (for she has gone no further) and her promises to reform. They resemble the Governor and his Lady in *The Spanish Wives*, in social class and style of speech as well as in their relationship. She has been tempted to intrigue; he, unlike the other men in this group, genuinely loves his wife: it is Mary Pix's usual requirement for a compatible marriage. None of this material is handled sentimentally, in spite of the usual critical assumptions about plays in this period. The men and women fight, scold, berate, and insult one another; the women stage fainting fits, weep, and make a burlesque of sentimental and romantic scenes, and both men and women spend a lot of time ducking into and out of closets, chests, beds, and doors. When Lady Loveman enters the apartment, disguised as a man to hide from her husband (IV, pp. 39–40), she tweaks Dandle's nose, then draws her sword and chases both men offstage for giving a woman (herself) a hard time. In all of this action it takes close reading to determine that no one goes to bed with anyone; on a busy stage there is hardly time for the audience to draw breath, let alone experience boredom because there are no scenes of successful illicit love.

While Sir James is in jail for debt, his new wife and his mother conspire to punish him for his licentious and self-indulgent life. He is led to believe that his new wife is a whore and is also penniless; then his mother sends word that she has disinherited him. Through these bizarre reversals of fortune he pretends indifference, as if, like Manly, his experience of the world makes these kinds of betrayals (by women) inevitable and not likely to get him down. Sir James is finally overcome, however, by the supposed death of his virtuous cousin Valentine, who is said to have been killed in a duel on Sir James's behalf. It is only after this loss that Sir James appears to be completely remorseful, and when Angelica and the others enter to tell him that his problems are imaginary, he promises to give up whoring and gaming. Mary Pix's plain dealer has not been betrayed by women after all, in spite of his deserts and expectations. But as much as Sir James loved him, Valentine was never able to persuade his friend to a more rational life; that is presented as the result of Lady Bellmont and Angelica's trickery. The jail scene in which he confesses his change of heart to the two women is protracted and seems, at least in text form, to be emotionally somewhat improbable. I believe, however, that Pix was attempting to create the reform the age required as well as repeating the changed assumptions about women that her plays uniformly argue.

All the genuine vices and follies of society in this play belong to the urban world; Angelica and Lady Bellmont have the same country background that Lady Landsworth and Bellinda share. Even Sir James, like the hero of *The Relapse*, is more able to behave well in the country than in town; the opening scene shows him at his country home behaving like a sensible man and patron of the arts. He pensions a fawning (and bad) poet (whom he excoriates as much for his flattery as his poor verse) to get rid of him and stop his pen. He lives so modestly that Valentine teases him for denying himself pleasure. The more wealthy the urban residents are, the more vicious they appear to be. While the "cits" are merely vulgar and foolish, Lady Gaylove and Lord Courtall are corrupt in both foolish and serious ways. In Act III of the play, for example, Lady Loveman proposes a visit to the theater as an amusement. She says that her citizen-turned-knight husband never goes there (implying that he has no cultured or leisure-class tastes). But Lady Gaylove refuses; the playhouse is so innocent, and perhaps so little in the upper-class mode these days, that it bores her; she only goes when she has "the Flatus" (III, p. 29), that is, to break wind. No genuine viciousness here, only total vulgarity. In this tiny particular, as in general, Pix's portrayals of female faults are not simple stereotypes applied to the whole sex, but the specific failings of individual human beings. She does not, however, make a case for immuring women in the country to improve them or protect them from corruption as parents do in such Restoration models as *The Man of Mode*; her women, unlike Sir James, do not abandon good sense, nor, like Loveless, do they become corrupt as soon as they get close to the money and fleshpots of London. The country is where an education into good sense, good manners, and self-esteem can occur for the young and naive Marina. It is where a woman like Lady Landsworth or Angelica develops the character she maintains ever afterwards. Excursions into town can then be taken without great loss, but, as Lady Bellmont is at pains to point out, without great pleasure either. The increasingly commercial urban world of William's and Anne's courts and the Whig and Tory financiers was undoubtedly (in 1703) already approaching the corruption we associate with such men as Harley, Bolingbroke, and Walpole. In this most explicit of her gradually intensifying attacks on the vices of London society, Pix anticipates some later plays and echoes such prose pieces of the past decade as Thomas Wright's *Country Conversations* (1693), a kind of moral dialogue comparing country and city life.[58]

Nevertheless, Pix's weapon against this world is not didacticism, but comedy, and she separates the nonurban world and the world of intelligent and educated women from the corruption of this age in ways her male peers did not. For example, Colley Cibber's successful play of the same period, *The Careless Husband* (first produced in December, 1704), takes place at Windsor, then a rural retreat twenty miles from London.[59] Residence at Windsor fails to separate virtue from vice in any way. London is acknowledged by the "witty" heroine, Lady Betty Modish, to be the headquarters for fashion and therefore a desirable source for those ideas and accessories which give women their only power, the power to attract and hold men. All of the other characters are also part-time London inhabitants, using the country as a place of sexual pursuit and conquest. Even the virtuous and long-suffering wife, Lady Easy (obviously a spiritual twin to Cibber's Amanda), wants only to reform her husband so that she may attract him and persuade him to love her. Where and how they live are not moral questions that concern her. The cynical conversation among the men turns upon Lord Foppington's design in leaving London, when Lord Morelove says to him, "But I thought, my lord, your business now at Windsor had been your design upon a woman of quality" (II, ii, p. 41). Other references to sexual pursuit in the play suggest that the men go where the women are, and that city morals and country life are pretty much the same. Cibber's mocking references from the Restoration tradition to milkmaids, country-foolish husbands—who don't know which men their wives are sleeping with—and "the cherry-cheek charms of my Lord Bishop's great fat daughter in the country" (III, p. 66), are spoken primarily by Lord Foppington, as if to emphasize his nature as a man of fashion. The rest of the play, apart from the usual topical comments on contemporary mores, is concerned with picturing all love relationships as power struggles between men and women, with the final victory in each combat going to the "virtuous" partner. It describes social norms and social conduct, but does not judge them; neither does the play distinguish the will to power or the will to virtue by gender: both men and women share or lack these qualities equally. Cibber is not concerned to make any kind of point about the virtues or vices of a particular way of living or about a social class or gender; and the emotional climate of the play, heavy in describing the reformed marriage of the Easys, almost vaudevillian in the scenes of sexual pursuit, reflects his lack of consistent moral perspective. In both these respects, Mary Pix's comedies are profoundly different.

The Different Widows was the only one of Mary Pix's comedies in which neither Elizabeth Barry nor Anne Bracegirdle is known to have taken part and was her last theatrical effort until after the opening of the new theater in the Haymarket, designed and constructed by Vanbrugh for Betterton's company in 1705. Milhous's history of the Lincoln's Inn Fields Company suggests some of the uncertainties of production for straight drama during the years 1704 and 1705: "These years saw the appearance of the multiple bill; the afterpiece tradition began to get established; and extraneous entertainments get a real stranglehold on the theatre. . . . The question became not which theatre would dominate but whether the London audience would support straight plays."[60] During this suspension of dramatic writing, Pix's time seems to have taken up with other literary activity. In 1704 she is known to have published *Violenta*, a verse translation of one of the stories from the *Decameron*;[61] she was also mentioned, under her literary pseudonym, Clio, in the 1704 "New Session of the Poets" in which Garth was nominated as the next poet laureate.[62] She had written some dedicatory verses for Bevil Higgons's *The Generous Conqueror* in 1703;[63] it is possible she was involved in other poetic enterprises of which we have no record. In the eight years between 1696 and 1704, Pix had been continuously active in theatrical work with ten plays written and produced. None of her work was extremely bad or more than modestly successful; it was evidently a meager living. Her career, along with those of her chief dramatic sponsors, Barry and Bracegirdle, was winding down.

Perhaps unexpectedly, the opening of Vanbrugh's extravagant new theater in April, 1705, marked the end of a period of theatrical transition that had sheltered them all. As Genest described it, "The new Theatre in the Hay market did not answer—it was soon found that almost every proper quality and convenience of a good Theatre had been sacrificed, or neglected, to show the spectator a vast triumphal piece of architecture."[64] Part of the problem with the new Queen's Theatre was evidently its acoustic properties.[65] Voices echoed and were lost in its great expanse; spoken drama could scarcely be heard or understood. Milhous details problems created for the company in another way by Vanbrugh's plan to mount Italian opera in the new theater. The new idea of importing Italian singers for *The Loves of Ergasto* did not succeed: "Vanbrugh suffered a humiliating misfire with his imported novelty—and then found that he had nothing to fall back on. . . . Clearly the Haymarket owners had no season planned beyond their hastily arranged opera." In fact, as Milhous suggests, "Vanbrugh moved the company in before the theatre was fully rigged and operational."[66] In May, 1705, after a scramble to mount some revivals "in old Cloaths," as Downes says in his history of the company, Mary Pix's new tragedy, *The Conquest of Spain*, was "the first new Play acted there" but did not last, closing on the sixth day.[67] No cast list remains to us and no response to the play exists in Jacob's *Poetical Register*; Genest noted that "Mrs. Pix is greatly indebted to the old play *All's Lost by Lust*, by Rowley (1633)," but that "Rowley's play, with all its faults is the better of the two."[68] So unsatisfactory overall was the spring season in the Haymarket theater that Lincoln's Inn Fields was reopened for use in the summer of 1705 "till Her Majesty's Theatre in the Hay-Market be intirely finish'd."[69] From this time until the reunion of the acting companies was accomplished in 1708, Vanbrugh's leadership seems to have alternated between a desire for this reunion and a renewed frenzy of competition. He was also changing his managerial relationship with both theaters and actors during this time. The result of any reunion would inevitably mean a reduction in the number of actors employed and obviously a reduced market for new play scripts; from 1705 onward it seems likely that a change in their circumstances must have been anticipated by everyone working in the theater.[70]

Mary Pix's theatrical career ended in June, 1706, with the performance of her last known play, another Spanish farce, *Adventures in Madrid*. It was produced at the new Queen's Theatre with Barry and Bracegirdle in important roles and the comedian Pack as the servant, Jo. The prologue to the play mentions Marlborough's victories over Louis XIV, perhaps a wistful analogy to the struggle between the theaters, and the body of the play includes Pix's earlier targets: jealous husbands, the corrupt Spanish Catholic priesthood, old husband/young wife marriages, and intrigues designed and carried on by women working in concert as mistress and maid or as friends. There are some attacks on corruption in aristocratic circles and at court, slightly more pointed, perhaps, since the play was set in Spain, but in such a context they do not seem very seriously meant:

> *Guzman*: Why, have ye no pimps in England then?
> *Jo*: Yes, marry have we; but they have other employments than yours. They are in no fear of the stab or the strapado. There's a pimp dines with a Lord, nay, often comes himself to preferment by his vocation, and is only called a friend to love, one who delights in doing good offices, and desires when parties meet tête a tête, there should be a right understanding between them.
>
> (II, pp. 32–33)

The play is not otherwise very interesting and does not show any particular advance in construction or subtlety over her earlier Spanish play, although it is more comic and less cautious in dialogue and innuendo:

> *Gomez*: Why haven't we Eunuchs in Spain? I say, why have we no Eunuchs?
> *Laura*: We have abundance of Old Men, and that's much the same thing.
>
> (I, p. 12)

This farce also places more emphasis than *The Spanish Wives* upon liberty as a guiding principle of life. It is not just for unhappy wives, but a general benefit for everyone:

> *Laura*: 'Tis liberty's each mortal's chief delight
> The sovereign good to which all plead a right,

My friend when liberty and love inspires
We cannot fail to compass our desires.

(I, p. 15)

England is described as a very paradise for wives because of the degree of liberty they are allowed, but the lovers have no objection to that—even the men seem to find the idea attractive. At the end of the play all the happy couples of whatever social rank leave for England. Given the circumstances of production at the Haymarket theater, the audience's taste for spectacle in this time, and the far from exciting script, it is not surprising that Judith Milhous should describe this last effort as a failure, although Genest says, "on the whole it is a good play."[71]

In 1706, Mary Pix was forty years old. She was widowed and, so far as we know, childless, neither wealthy nor renowned as a writer. Whatever the advantages of the support she had probably received as a playwright from Elizabeth Barry and Anne Bracegirdle during her career, it may have cost her more than she gained. She certainly had steady employment; she was protected from the worst effects of the Collier controversy and its aftermath; as long as Barry survived, she survived as well. But I believe that her real gift was for comedy and that by working at Lincoln's Inn Fields she lost an opportunity to develop her talent in ways most suited to her.

Many of her characters in both comedy and tragedy were specifically tailored (it seems) to the skills and interests of those two great actresses, Barry and Bracegirdle. That other performers and producers did not find her plays generally useful after Barry's retirement cannot be entirely attributed to their quality. For while romantic tragedy was going out of style and hardly survived the retirement of its most famous actress at the end of 1709, Pix's comedy scripts are genuinely funny, well written, and well crafted. Only her first two plays, a historical tragedy and a comedy-farce, written *without* specific actors in mind, entered the repertory. Yet these are not by any means her best works; they are novice efforts. It was understood that the most skillful comic actors and actresses were to be found at Drury Lane during the period in which Pix was writing, so the feud with the Patent Company that originally drove her to the refuge of Lincoln's Inn Fields and the friendship of that company may have limited the full development of her comic talent.[72] She was evidently friendly with Congreve—*The Innocent Mistress* shows the degree to which she was influenced by him, but he took no further part in theatrical life as a playwright after 1700. And it is after all the skillful and influential actor who is able to say to a writer, "Try this," or "I don't think that will work, but something like this might." Although she was friendly with Peter Motteux, who wrote prologues and epilogues for her, and with Catharine Trotter and Susanna Centlivre, who also wrote plays for the Lincoln's Inn Fields Company, as a woman she was hardly likely to be able to work consistently with the circle of men who drank and swapped stories and did reviews for one another at Will's or the RoseTavern or the Blue Posts. Furthermore, her comedies are not the new type of psychological drama being developed at this time by Vanbrugh and Cibber. Pix's interest was almost more sociological in some ways than psychological, and her interest in character was expressed in more oblique ways than theirs (perhaps because it was more subversive): she used bits of dialogue, comic situations, subtle changes in the circumstances or attitudes of her dominant female characters.

Perhaps, too, plays written with women at center stage, about women as main characters rather than objects of sexual pursuit or as foils to or victims of men, were not yet acceptable to London audiences. Slight supporting evidence for this idea may be found in Genest's comment on *The Different Widows*, when he says that "Sir James Bellmont is a good character, the rest of this comedy has not much to recommend it."[73] A curious observation, as if it was not evident to the critic how relatively unimportant to the action Sir James is, compared with the two widows and the heroine who wins him, or as if that shift in interest is a flaw in the structure. The limited run of Susanna Centlivre's *The Basset Table* (1705), a play about women, suggests that this may indeed have been a problem. Up until 1714, in fact, Centlivre's only truly successful comedies were two dominated by the male central characters: *The Gamester* (1704) and *The Busie Body* (1709).[74]

Apart from her advancing age and the approaching loss of her theatrical home, Mary Pix suffered throughout her short career from a general hostility expressed toward her almost from her earliest days as a playwright. Some of the actors and writers whom we know to have been ill-disposed toward her were still very active at Drury Lane in 1706. Certainly the first union of the companies, in the autumn of 1706, was one in which she could have expected to receive no warm welcome.[75] That she aroused the kind of jealous resentment described by Nancy Cotton in her chapter on "The Salic Law of Wit," is confirmed both by her disappearance from theatrical history during the past 250 years and by the little digs at her which do survive in such diverse sources as *The Female Wits* (1697); Gildon's edition of Langbaine's *Lives*, in which she is the only female writer maligned; *Animadversions on Mr. Congreve's Late Answer to Mr. Collier* (now usually attributed to her old enemy Powell), in which she is rudely described as a "She-Thing";[76] the *Comparison between the Two Stages*, in which it is stated that her "Muse was wont to hobble like a young Negro Wench, that had just learnt to wear Shoes and Stockins";[77] and in an odd reference from a satire of 1701 called "The Town Display'd," in which she is condemned (along with Peter Motteux, Charles Gildon, and Catharine Trotter) to be "Forgotten now, and in Futurity."[78] That last anonymous threat seems to have been all too successful. Yet it is a curious instance of taking a blunderbuss to silence a woman's feeble pen. If Mary Pix's work was really that poor and that unimportant, why bother? She did not, apparently, inspire the kind of personal rancor associated by her enemies with Delariviere Manley. In *The Female Wits*, in fact, she is described as "fat," but also as "a good sociable well-natured companion."[79] She seems from the tone of her dedications to have been modest and unassuming; no real controversy except over the plagiarism of her work is known of her. Judging from the dedications of her later work to such high-ranking women as the Duchess of Bolton and the Countess of Burlington, she had some standing in her lifetime as a writer. One can then only speculate, with the slender evidence available and what we can know of the theater in her time.

The dates of the published attacks upon Pix are perhaps one kind of clue to this hostility. In each of these years she had one and sometimes two of her plays produced. She was that anomaly among women writers of her time—successful, minimally so, but successful. And up to the success of Centlivre's *Gamester* in 1704, she was the only writer of her sex to make a living in the theater since the death of Aphra Behn. Manley was, by the end of the seventeenth century, a journalist and budding novelist; Trotter was having occasional plays acted, but apart from the appeal made by her beauty and decorum, she showed no particular literary talent; there were no others able to succeed with more than one play. Aphra Behn was safely out of the way; her work produced revenue for the actors, but her name did not even have to appear on the playbills. Where Pix trod successfully, others—it was to be feared—might some day follow; and of course for a few years they did: Susanna Centlivre, Eliza Haywood, Mary Davys. Centlivre seems to have acknowledged a genuine debt to her predecessor by dedicating a benefit of *The Busie Body* in May, 1709, to Mary Pix's estate.[80]

For the reader who goes to the texts of Pix's comedies, another reason for the attacks upon her writing appears. Her plays were about women: ordinary, middle-class, sometimes middle-aged women, not about men. She had male characters in the plays, but her real interest was not in the men at all. She had funny, meaty parts for three, four, sometimes five, actresses, in an era when plays tended to list two—occasionally three—substantial roles for women. The women are not young, doll-like beauties nor aging and bitter cast mistresses; they are independent, funny, sometimes bawdy, often powerful; they fit no traditional mold for the late seventeenth century and their creator *likes* them, which for her time may have been the most radical idea of all. In a time when there was considerable new writing being done by women in varied genres, Mary Pix stood—with the help of friends and associates and despite her enemies—where no other woman of her day managed to stand. There she remains: stubbornly committed to her unique perceptions of women in the post-Restoration theater and the comic vision which describes them.

IN SEARCH OF MRS. PILKINGTON

DIANA M. A. RELKE

In 1747, after nine colorful years in London, Mrs. Laetitia Pilkington returned to her native Ireland to write her memoirs. She was not the first "lady of adventure" to turn autobiographer. That honor, according to Donald Stauffer, goes to Madame d'Aulnoy, who published the *Memoirs of her own life* in 1690. These *Memoirs* "may well have furnished the model for the confessions of injured females which poured out from eighteenth-century printing-presses." Stauffer does not take Madame d'Aulnoy very seriously as an autobiographer because he cannot determine "what part of her confessions is literally true."[1] Her *Memoirs* are fictionalized autobiography—the mirror image of that other popular eighteenth-century form, autobiographical fiction, a strange combination of "half-fiction and half-fact [that is] acceptable neither to the historian nor to the literary critic."[2]

Madame d'Aulnoy's purpose—and consequently the convention of the genre she initiated—"is to furnish a cautionary tale as to how to preserve one's reputation," Stauffer explains. Her "conviction that the world is wrong and that the outcast autobiographer is suffering unjustly after impeccable conduct, will not be uncommon among other unfortunate women who turned an honest penny, at last, by writing their memoirs."[3] Included among the other "unfortunate women" who carried on in the tradition were Delariviere ("Mary") Manley (*The Adventures of Rivella,* 1714); the actresses Charlotte Charke (1755), George Anne Bellamy (1785), and Mary Robinson (1801); and the lively Con Phillips, whose *Apology for the conduct of Mrs. Teresia Constantia Phillips* (1749) was compared to the *Memoirs* of Mrs. Laetitia Pilkington in a pamphlet written by "an Oxford Scholar."[4]

Mrs. Pilkington's stated purpose is the conventional one:

And I am the more inclined to proceed, in that I think the Story
may be instructive to the *Female* Part of my Readers, to teach them that
Reputation
Is the immediate Jewel of their Souls,
And that the Loss of it
Will make them poor indeed!
(Othello.)
So that I propose myself, not as an Example, but a Warning to them; that
by my Fall, they may stand the more secure.[5]

However, as the *Memoirs* proceed we find that her true purpose is quite different
from the stated one. Scattered throughout her three volumes—two of which
were published in 1748, the last, posthumously, in 1754—are veiled and not-
so-veiled admissions that she is motivated by poverty, revenge, and a desire for
literary recognition. These motives, however, are not generally recognized as
the true purpose of serious autobiography, and consequently the *Memoirs,* like
most of the efforts by women in this genre, have never been fully appreciated as
legitimate literary self-portraiture. But poverty, revenge, and literary ambition
suggest the specific terms of Mrs. Pilkington's autobiography, and it seems
only fair to judge the *Memoirs* on their own terms. If we do so, we find that the
Memoirs—whatever their relationship to fact—tell us as much about their author as do the carefully controlled and censored male life-writings that dictate
the standards of "great" autobiography.[6] Indeed, Mrs. Pilkington's departures
from the kind of truth that satisfies both historian and literary critic are the
most revealing aspects of the *Memoirs,* for in order to tell the truth Mrs. Pilkington must resort to lies.

Donald Stauffer and other traditional critics and theorists of autobiography
who express uneasiness with or contempt for life-writers who tamper with facts
come by their opinions honestly. Fidelity to fact as an important criterion of
autobiography goes back to Samuel Johnson who, as Stauffer writes, "changed
the course of English biography by his written and spoken observations even
more than by his own practice."[7] In the *Idler* essay for November 24, 1759,
Johnson wrote:

The writer of his own life has at least the first qualification of an Historian, the knowledge of the truth; and though it may be plausibly ob-
jected that his temptations to disguise it are equal to his opportunities of
knowing it, yet I cannot but think that impartiality may be expected with
equal confidence from him that relates the passages of his own life, as
from him that delivers the transactions of another.
 . . . he that speaks of himself has no motive to Falshood or Partiality
except Self-love, by which all have so often been betrayed, that all are on
the watch against its artifices. He that writes an Apology for a single

Action, to confute an Accusation, or recommend himself to Favour, is indeed always to be suspected of favouring his own cause.[8]

Johnson's zeal for "truth" has been handed down through generations of critics and life-writers; Boswell's almost fanatical pursuit of factual detail is well known. Johnson's shadow still loomed large over the critical canon in the early twentieth century; for example, echoes of Johnson can be heard in Arthur Melville Clark's *Autobiography: Its Genesis and Phases* (1935):

> It demands a mind of the most perfect integrity and one under an iron discipline to be aware of and then to resist the temptation to create. Even the mind which can be trusted not to falsify the main lines of life will succumb to an artistic instinct for the adjustment and bettering of the details. There are very few who realize how in absolute truth there is the highest art of all.[9]

There seems to be little doubt in Clark's mind that "truth" and "fact" are synonymous. What is more interesting, however, is the implication that "artistic instinct" is not necessarily a desirable quality in an autobiographer—indeed, that this artistic instinct can prevent the autobiographer from creating "the highest art of all."

Roy Pascal's *Design and Truth in Autobiography*, published in 1960, demonstrates a cautious shift away from the traditional demand for adherence to factual detail and explores the elusiveness of truth and the undependability of memory. Pascal recognizes that memory is selective and that the autobiographer's truth as he experiences it within may differ substantially from objective fact. Nevertheless he believes that "The most frequent cause of failure in autobiography is an untruthfulness which arises from the desire to appear admirable, especially when the standard set is conventional propriety. Even here, however, . . . the purpose of many autobiographers may quite legitimately justify them in ignoring whole aspects of their being."[10] Although he apparently does not recognize that "the desire to appear admirable" is a telling characteristic, Pascal does make an important connection between purpose and truth in autobiography, a connection which he explains as follows:

> We have . . . to define what sort of truth is meant, and this we can discover only in relation to the author's general intention. It will not be an objective truth, but the truth in the confines of a limited purpose, a purpose that grows out of the author's life and imposes itself on him as his specific quality, and thus determines his choice of events and the manner of his treatment and expression.[11]

This careful consideration of the relationship between purpose and truth does not solve the problem of fact versus fiction in autobiography; it does, however, state the age-old problem in a new way and suggest new critical directions. Neither does the present study attempt to solve the problem but rather "to define what sort of truth is meant," by examining Mrs. Pilkington's *Memoirs* "in relation to the author's general intention."

The undeniable core of fact contained in the *Memoirs* can be summarized in a few brief sentences. The *Memoirs* tell of Mrs. Pilkington's marriage to the Reverend Matthew Pilkington somewhere between the ages of thirteen and sixteen, the steady deterioration of their relationship, and their final separation when she was around twenty-five years old. They go on to tell of her attempts to support herself, first in Dublin and later in London, through ghostwriting for male customers who passed her poems and love letters off as their own. She found that her chief competition in this business was her husband; both she and Matthew were simultaneously supplying the painter James Worsdale with poems, plays, and opera libretti. She tells of contemplating suicide and of spending nine weeks in debtor's prison for default of a week's rent. The actor Colley Cibber, a special friend to her in these London years, took up a collection from among her aristocratic male acquaintances: the sum was enough to buy her freedom and to set up a shop selling prints along with her literary services. When the print shop failed, she blackmailed an old enemy by threatening to expose him in her forthcoming *Memoirs,* and thus earned just enough money to get her back to Dublin. She arrived in time to prevent her husband's illegal marriage—the Divorce Act permitting remarriage in cases like the Pilkingtons' was still ten years in the future; Matthew had told his intended bride that Laetitia was dead. Mrs. Pilkington never managed to recover her reputation; not surprisingly, Matthew had better luck. Two weeks after she died, at the age of thirty-eight, just days after completing her third volume, Matthew married his mistress and settled down to a respectable life as the vicar of Donabate and St. Mary's in Dublin and the author of an influential *Dictionary of Painters.*

The appearance of the first two volumes of the *Memoirs* touched off a pamphlet war between Mrs. Pilkington and her husband. This publicity did much to ensure the immediate popularity of the *Memoirs,* for the early eighteenth century had an insatiable appetite for scurrilous and scandalous autobiography. But more important to their success were the author's anecdotes of Jonathan Swift, with whom the Pilkingtons had been on intimate terms during the early years of their marriage. She sprinkled these anecdotes throughout her lively volumes along with her own poetry. Mrs. Pilkington's lack of credibility *vis-à-vis* the details of her own life notwithstanding, these anecdotes describing the extremely eccentric behavior of the elderly Swift ensured a continued interest among the literati well into the latter half of the eighteenth century. These anecdotes were thoroughly exploited by many magazines and newspapers, and in 1751, a volume containing the anecdotes and entitled *The Celebrated Mrs. Pilkington's Jests, or the Cabinet of Wit and Humor* was published; this volume went into a second edition, with additions, in 1765. Even as late as 1780 we find Mrs. Thrale comparing Mrs. Pilkington's anecdotes with a corroborating account of Swift by Alexander Pope.[12]

Indeed, the veracity of the anecdotes has never been seriously disputed, for, as the *Dictionary of National Biography* states, "the internal evidence of their authenticity is quite conclusive."[13] However, although Mrs. Pilkington continued as the chief source of information about Swift's later years—indeed, in 1853 Thackeray made extensive use of the anecdotes in his *English Humourists of the Eighteenth Century*—the *Memoirs* as an autobiography did not sustain interest for very long. The reading public was beginning to demand more sexual virtue from its women writers, as the following comments by Elizabeth Montagu suggest:

> I have read the first volume of Mrs. Pilkington. She has a pretty genius for poetry, a turn of wit and satire and vanity—It is often said that Wit is a dangerous quality; it is there meant that it is an offensive weapon, and is a perilous thing in society; but Wit in women is apt to have other bad consequences; like a sword without a scabbard it wounds the wearer and provokes assailants. I am sorry to say the generality of women who have excelled in wit have failed in chastity; perhaps it inspires too much confidence in the possessor, and raises an inclination in the men towards them without inspiring an esteem so that they are more attacked and less guarded than other women.[14]

And so we have it from no less an authority than the "Queen of the Blues" that "inspiring an esteem" in men was becoming a much more effective female literary tactic than displaying "a pretty genius for poetry, a turn of wit and satire and vanity." Wit in a woman could be as self-destructive as a lapse in chastity, and so it is hardly surprising that as an autobiographer Mrs. Pilkington dropped into relative obscurity and remained there for the whole of the nineteenth century.

In 1914, there appeared a six-volume edition of Swift's correspondence edited by F. Elrington Ball. The many references in these volumes to Swift's relationship with the Pilkingtons were almost certainly responsible for the brief revival of interest in the *Memoirs*. No fewer than four lengthy critiques had appeared by 1937.[15] Unlike Mrs. Montagu, these later critics sense something in Mrs. Pilkington capable of "inspiring an esteem." "As with all long-dead persons," writes Iris Barry in her introduction to a 1928 reissue of the *Memoirs*, "her character is more interesting than her morals."[16] Mrs. Pilkington's courage and humor make her worthy of reassessment, although her fairly obvious departures from the truth make it difficult for these early twentieth-century critics to take her seriously as an autobiographer. These commentators are hampered in part by their belief that a good autobiographer never alters the facts of his/her life. For Lord Ponsonby, writing in 1937, the *Memoirs* are largely a "formless jumble peppered with exaggerations, and, probably, falsehoods."[17] He prefers those parts of Mrs. Pilkington's volumes that "can be authenticated apart from her own confessions."[18] The opening sentence of Walter and Clare Jerrold's lengthy article of 1929 also reflects this concern with "falsehood": "How can a reader discriminate, when reading a biography, between fact and fiction, or between actual fact and that which is embroidered by the mind which relates it?"[19] They then go on without bothering to discriminate, for Iris Barry before them had taken the trouble to do so.

Barry tackles the problem head-on by attempting to determine exactly what can and what cannot be verified in Mrs. Pilkington's account of the events of her life. Her introduction is a thoroughgoing piece of scholarship which makes use of a wide variety of sources in support of the main facts of the narrative. For example, Barry demonstrates that if Matthew Pilkington did not commit every crime of which his wife accuses him, he was certainly more than capable of doing so. However, Barry can find no external evidence in support of Mrs. Pilkington's claim to sexual virtue. Barry calls her a "silly little thing to protest so much and fight so ardently to keep up appearance."[20] But it is not only her falsehoods that make her a poor autobiographer:

> Laetitia mentions nothing of the Rebellion [of 1745]. Like too many authors of "Memoirs," she forgets that incidents which were commonplaces of current talk in 1748 might be thrilling two hundred years later. She flicks off, for instance, the remark that Harry Carey, along with her husband, was the most assiduous literary ghost or "poetical stockjobber" as she calls it, for Worsdale, and never dreamt how much we should have preferred a little gossip about the author of "Sally in our Alley" to diatribes against Bishops! And for which theatres did this "sad digressive writer" write Worsdale's operas—Haymarket, Lincoln's Inn Fields, or where?[21]

Clearly, Barry has some definite ideas about what constitutes good autobiography. Mrs. Pilkington's *Memoirs* lack the attention to political and historical detail that characterizes what we have come to accept as "great" autobiography. Edward Gibbon, J. J. Rousseau, J. S. Mill, and even Colley Cibber are careful to locate themselves in history because they have a sense of audience that reaches many generations into the future. Unlike these men, Mrs. Pilkington fails to locate herself solidly in time and space. Given her failure to meet these criteria, it is hardly surprising that she has been consigned to the footnotes of Swift biographies.

Of all Mrs. Pilkington's early twentieth-century commentators, only Virginia Woolf has more interest in the *Memoirs* as autobiography than she has in the anecdotes of Swift. However, her article, which was included in her *Common Reader* in 1925, also exhibits some uneasiness with Mrs. Pilkington's unconvincing defense of her moral virtue. Woolf deals with this problem by assuming a tone of mock tragedy which effectively undercuts Mrs. Pilkington's strongest claims to sincerity. Woolf finds Laetitia Pilkington

> so imbued with the old traditions of her sex that she wrote, as ladies talk, to give pleasure. Throughout her *Memoirs,* we can never forget that it is her wish to entertain, her unhappy fate to sob. Dabbing her eyes and controlling her anguish, she begs us to forgive an odious breach of manners which only the suffering of a lifetime, the intolerable persecutions of Mr. P———n, the malignant, she must say the h———h, spite of Lady C———t can excuse. For who should know better than the Earl of Killmallock's great-granddaughter that it is the part of a lady to hide her sufferings? Thus Laetitia is in the great tradition of English women of letters. It is her duty to entertain; it is her instinct to conceal.[22]

In spite of the fun she has at Laetitia's expense, Woolf makes several important points that anticipate a more contemporary approach to women's autobiography. She points out Mrs. Pilkington's tendency to define herself in terms of her relationship to powerful male figures—in this case her aristocratic ancestor. This suggests a shift in emphasis away from the men themselves and toward the roles they play in helping Laetitia create a sense of her own identity. Woolf also recognizes that Mrs. Pilkington's version of events is controlled by internalized gender conventions, and, more important, that this quality is not so much a personal failing as it is a characteristic of the female tradition in English literature. Finally, as Woolf's opposition of the terms "duty" and "instinct" suggests, the *Memoirs* are characterized by conflict: for example, how much of what the author would rather conceal must she reveal in order to make her book sell, make herself credible, make herself socially acceptable in the eyes of her readers? All these points suggest that a shift of critical emphasis from "factual" to psychological truth is in order.

What we need to do to get at the psychological truth contained in the *Memoirs* is lay to rest the negative criticisms of these early twentieth-century commentators and investigate the possibility that what have been perceived as Mrs. Pilkington's faults as a writer actually help her to achieve her ends. We must begin by reexamining the criteria of autobiography in terms of the realities of women's lives. Recent feminist attempts to trace the history of the female tradition in autobiography are instructive, for feminist critics question the appropriateness of the criteria applied to women's life-writings. Second, we must consider Mrs. Pilkington's perception of herself in the traditional female roles of daughter, wife, and mother. The ways in which she copes with her failure to fulfill social expectations in these roles reveals far more about her character than the fact of failure itself. Finally, because the roles of daughter, wife, and mother were the only acceptable ones for women in the eighteenth century, we need to examine the ways in which Mrs. Pilkington creates an identity for herself outside these traditional roles. In spite of the fact that she is forced out of the domestic role, she cannot escape her sense of entrapment in it, and she cannot move into new roles without first envisioning them through the characters who people her narrative.

In her introduction to a collection of articles entitled *Women's Autobiography* (1980), Estelle Jelinek broadly outlines some of the characteristics of male autobiography against which women's literary self-portraiture has been measured and found wanting. One observation in particular is revealing in terms of the Rebellion of 1745 and other "commonplaces of current talk in 1748" that Iris Barry misses so much in Mrs. Pilkington's *Memoirs:*

> The consensus among critics is that good autobiography not only focuses on its author but also reveals his connectedness to the rest of society; it is representative of his times, a mirror of his era. This criterion is adequately supported by the many male autobiographies which concentrate on chronicling the progress of their authors' professional or intellectual lives, usually in the affairs of the world, and their life studies are for the most part success stories. . . .
>
> On the other hand, women's autobiographies rarely mirror the establishment history of their times. They emphasize to a much lesser extent the public aspects of their lives, the affairs of the world, or even their careers, and concentrate instead on their personal lives—domestic details, family difficulties, close friends, and especially people who influenced them.[23]

It is not Mrs. Pilkington's purpose to establish her "connectedness to the rest of society" but to reveal her alienation from it. It is true that one searches the *Memoirs* in vain for dates and public events that would help to locate her in time and space. But the consequence of this is that her story has a kind of timelessness, and by focusing largely on the Swift material—material which is attractive to critics because it does locate Mrs. Pilkington within the framework of literary history—her commentators obscure the timelessness of her statement. Swift was just one of a series of father figures who fall into the category of "friends and . . . people who influenced" her. As we shall see, her perception of herself as the spiritual daughter of several rather unconventional men gave her at least some sense of the validity of her own unconventionality.

In her study of the relationship between eighteenth-century autobiography and fiction, Patricia Meyer Spacks builds on Roy Pascal's theory of autobiography as a reflection of the truth as experienced by the autobiographer rather than as a chronicling of historical fact. Spacks defines autobiography as an affirmation of identity and discusses at length the extent to which autobiographers depend upon both memory and imagination. She examines eighteenth-century women's autobiography largely in terms of its function as defense: autobiographies like Mrs. Pilkington's, "in which the effort to assert a distinct identity seems a way to defend against the world's encroachments on the self," she writes, "suggest some attempt to invent a valid identity for defensive purposes."[24] This has special significance in terms of Mrs. Pilkington's version of her disastrous marriage. It was Matthew's failure to meet his marital responsibilities, she writes, which "determined me in the Design, of publickly vindicating my Innocence, and laying open, for universal Benefit, his unparallel'd Character" (3: 198). Indeed, the discrediting of Matthew's character is entirely dependent upon the vindication of her "Innocence." Spacks describes Matthew as a villain "of almost mythical proportions" manufactured by Laetitia "in order to justify [her] own expression of anger."[25] However, thanks to Barry's investigation of the incorrigible Matthew and our own contemporary understanding of the conditions of women's lives, it is hardly necessary to defend Mrs. Pilkington's feelings of rage. Trapped in the gender conventions of the age, she felt constrained to make herself be seen as conforming to every social convention governing female conduct; only then would her argument carry the force necessary to shift the blame for the destruction of her reputation to where it probably for the most part belonged.

But vindicating one's innocence in the eyes of the world is altogether different from establishing a self-image one can live with. Traditionally, autobiography is seen as the story of a personality unfolding and developing over time. This implies a one-directional, forward movement through life that begins with a set of aspirations and ends with their fulfillment. But Cynthia Pomerleau, writing on the development of women's autobiography in the seventeenth and eighteenth centuries, notes:

> The traditional view of women is antithetical to the crucial motive of autobiography—a desire to synthesize, to see one's life as an organic whole, to look back for a pattern. Women's lives are fragmented; they start as young women and are successively transformed from without into either spinsters, demimondaines, wives, mothers, or matriarchs. The process is not one of growth, of evolution; rather, they enter each stage as a failure of the previous stage. Earlier and more decisively than for a man, the curve of a woman's life is seen by herself and society to be one of deterioration and denigration. Men may mature, but women age.[26]

This observation seems appropriate to Mrs. Pilkington's *Memoirs,* for the shape of her life does indeed curve ever downward. She begins as the precocious child of a loving and supportive father and dies at thirty-eight, a notorious and impoverished "adventuress." That she is aware of the fragmented nature of her own identity is evident throughout the *Memoirs,* especially in the following passage:

> But I have been a Lady of Adventure, and almost every Day of my Life produces some new one: I am sure, I ought to thank my loving Husband for the Opportunity he has afforded me of seeing the World from the Palace to the Prison; for had he but permitted me to be what Nature certainly intended me for, a harmless houshold Dove, in all human Probability I should have rested contented with my humble Situation, and, instead of using a Pen, been employed with a Needle, to work for the little ones we might, by this time, have had.
>
> (2: 252)

The images of princess and prisoner, adventuress and housewife evoked by this passage hardly suggest a life perceivable as "an organic whole." In fact, the downward curve of Mrs. Pilkington's life moves through the roles of daughter, wife, mother, poet, professional companion, gentlewoman, businesswoman, beggar. Although this downward curve does suggest some kind of pattern, it is a pattern of disintegration rather than integration. Therefore, if the "crucial motive" of autobiography is, as Pomerleau claims, "a desire to synthesize," it is hardly surprising that where memory frustrates that desire Mrs. Pilkington resorts to invention. Aided by both imagination and memory, she attempts to write herself into existence, to fuse her fragmented identity into the "organic whole" she so desires. If any part of her notion of literary achievement is realized in the *Memoirs,* it is not in her poetry (with which she had hoped to win her fame), nor even in her anecdotes of Swift (with which she did). Rather, it is in this slightly fictionalized heroine whose courage and humor so fascinate her later critics.

Virginia Woolf, when she says of Laetitia that "it is her wish to entertain, her unhappy fate to sob," reminds us that the heroine of the *Memoirs* resembles the most popular heroine of eighteenth-century fiction. Richardson's Pamela writes for her own entertainment as well as that of half the characters in the novel (and Richardson's readers as well). Even when her copious tears threaten to dissolve the words on the page, she scribbles on. Pamela writes about her defense of her sexual virtue; Laetitia writes in defense of her claim to it. Pamela spends most of the novel trapped inside one or the other of Mr. B———'s houses; Laetitia's life is a series of imprisonments behind doors, gates, and prison bars—indeed, entrapment is a major metaphor in her narrative. However, this is where the the resemblance ends, for Pamela knows who she is, and it is that knowledge that keeps her "honest" (not to mention entirely unbelievable). Laetitia, however, is engaged in a quest for self through a gallery of characters, which includes her ancestors, family members, friends, and mysterious unnamed acquaintances. It is a gallery that often resembles a hall of mirrors. Through these mirror images combined with the images of entrapment and enclosure we get a glimpse of the kind of unity Mrs. Pilkington is seeking.

But it would be an oversimplification to put the *Memoirs* into the same category with *Pamela* or *Moll Flanders,* although Mrs. Pilkington's heroine does emerge as a curious combination of the two. Indeed, she impressed Virginia Woolf as "a very extraordinary cross between Moll Flanders and Lady Ritchie, between a rolling and rollicking woman of the town and a lady of breeding and refinement."[27] This incongruous duality is the result of the overlap between fact and fiction, the tension between Mrs. Pilkington's desire for the right to her own experience and her equally strong desire for credibility in the world. Throughout the *Memoirs* we find covert admissions of her lapse in chastity, halfhearted attempts to explain away compromising situations with men, and curious business transactions that read more like metaphors for sexual solicitation. (No doubt she is tempted into these veiled confessions in part by the knowledge that sexual scandal sells books.) It is this vacillation between the invented heroine of her story and the real-life Laetitia that Spacks's brief analysis fails to take into account. (Spacks also diminishes the profit motive.) This vacillation moves the *Memoirs* beyond Spacks's definition of eighteenth-century women's autobiography as simply defense, and demonstrates the ambivalence felt by women who are forced to live out the split between who they really are and the roles they are pressured into assuming.

Given that female identity has always been defined in terms of a woman's relationships with the men who control her existence, it is hardly surprising that female autobiographers focus so much attention on fathers, husbands, and sons. Mrs. Pilkington's story is largely one of rejection by the men in her life—a fact which helps to account for the number of men she treats as father figures in her *Memoirs*. This list of father figures begins, curiously enough, with a man she never met: her uncle, Sir John Meade, son of the Earl of Killmallock, a lawyer by profession, and an enormously proud man. In the opening pages of the *Memoirs* she relates a lengthy story about how Sir John is visited by a prospective client, Sir Edward Seymour, an excessively proud Englishman with a contempt for all things Irish. In an attempt to break Sir Edward's pride, Sir John rudely keeps him waiting for over an hour. When Sir Edward is finally admitted he engages Sir John's services and then "depart[s], full of Indignation at meeting with a Man as proud as himself" (1: 8). In the end Sir John wins his client's respect and admiration through a resounding victory in court on behalf of Sir Edward. Mrs. Pilkington is careful to explain in exactly what relationship she stands to this proud and accomplished gentleman. He is proof of the legacy of pride and gentility to which she is heir. His story also serves to demonstrate how intelligence and accomplishment excuse such faults as pride and rudeness. Interestingly, Sir John's story is immediately preceded in Mrs. Pilkington's narrative by her proud and haughty diatribe against all those who lack the Christian grace and charity to overlook her mistakes and shortcomings.

The father figure who exerts the greatest influence on Laetitia is, of course, her real father, Dr. Van Lewen, a Dublin obstetrician of Dutch birth. The story she tells about his support and encouragement of her education is interesting in terms of the later events of her life. "From my earliest Infancy," she writes, "I had a strong Disposition to Letters; but my Eyes being weak, after the Smallpox, I was not permitted to look at a Book; my Mother regarding more the Beauty of my Face, than the Improvement of my Mind" (1: 13). Despite the blows she received from her mother each time she asked to be told the names of the letters of the alphabet, she learned to read quickly. One day, when she was about five years old, her mother was away and Laetitia took advantage of the time to read aloud a page from *Alexander's Feast*. Her father, closeted in his study, heard the recitation and emerged. Laetitia was so frightened of his expected displeasure that she dropped the book and began to cry. But to her astonishment,

> Instead of the whipping, of which I stood in dread, he took me up in his Arms, and kissed me, giving me a whole Shilling, as a Reward, and told me, "He would give me another, as soon as I got a Poem by Heart," which he put into my Hand, and proved to be Mr. *Pope's* sacred Eclogue; which Task I performed before my Mother returned Home. They were both astonished at my Memory, and from that Day forward, I was permitted to read as much as I pleased; only my Father took care to furnish me with the best, and politest Authors; and took delight in explaining to me, whatever, by Reason of my tender Years, was above my Capacity of Understanding.
>
> (1: 15)

This intimate exchange of kisses and money between father and daughter comes to mind again and again, whenever she writes of her business transactions with the men who, like her father, paid her for the products of her wit and learning. This relationship between intimacy and money, which runs like a *leitmotiv* through the *Memoirs,* is part of what undermines her insistence upon her sexual virtue.

Laetitia's rejection of and triumph over her mother, who insisted upon the cultivation of her daughter's sexual power at the expense of her intellectual development, is also significant. As so much recent feminist scholarship has demonstrated, it is common for daughters to resent mothers who offer them only the model of their own narrow lives. Indeed, Laetitia even accused her mother of railroading her into a disastrous marriage:

> . . . as I approached towards Womanhood there was a new Scene opened to me; and by the Time I had looked on thirteen Years, I had almost as many Lovers; . . . no doubt but I should have been happily disposed of in Marriage, but that my Mother's capricious Temper made her reject every advantageous Proposal offered, and at last condemn me to the Arms of one of the greatest V——s, with Reverence to the Priesthood be it spoken, that ever was wrapt up in Crape.

(1: 16—17)

Not only did she repeat her mother's mistake of marrying downward and into straitened circumstances, she also chose a far less worthy husband than did her mother. Antagonism between mother and daughter resulted in their complete alienation from each other upon the death of Dr. Van Lewen. When Mrs. Pilkington's father lay dying of a stab wound, her mother tried to keep the news from her. But she found out and forced her way to her father's bedside and nursed him back to health, only to lose him a few days later to influenza.

Swift's delight in playing the role of stern literary father to women poets is reflected in the tremendous influence he had on the young Laetitia. She earned an introduction to him by writing a poem on the occasion of his birthday. It was during the first year of her marriage that they met, and Swift's response when she was introduced as Matthew Pilkington's wife was: "What . . . this poor little Child married! God help her, she is early engaged in Trouble" (1: 52). She became a frequent guest at the Deanery and endured his unmerciful teasing along with the pinches and blows he administered when she irritated him. He fanned the sparks of rivalry that were beginning to ignite between Laetitia and Matthew, who was also a poet, by declaring that on occasion she exhibited more wit and poetic facility than her husband.

Whatever the indignities she was forced to endure, she also had access to her famous friend's fertile mind. He read and discussed books with her, allowed her to read his private correspondence, and did his utmost to improve her English by pinching her each time she used an inelegant phrase. He encouraged her to read widely, and she did, as is evidenced by the hundreds of quotations from numerous authors sprinkled throughout her *Memoirs*. By her own admission she had a phenomenal memory, as the vast number and variety of these quoted passages demonstrate. Her conversations with Swift were no doubt responsible for the confidence with which she discusses the faults and virtues of some of the works she cites.

Mrs. Pilkington was also influenced by Swift's intense obsession with cleanliness. On one occasion he tricked her into removing her shoes in the hope of catching her with "broken Stockings, or foul Toes" (3: 148). On his first visit to her and Matthew, he inspected the house from garret to kitchen, for only "a Slut" would limit her housekeeping to the rooms where guests were entertained. Mrs. Pilkington was slightly tainted with this obsession, and throughout her *Memoirs* the strongest insults she can think to hurl are references to slovenly housekeeping and unclean personal habits.

The elderly Colley Cibber, another father figure, proved a good protector to Laetitia in her London years. Like her father, he encouraged her intellectual pursuits and gave her gifts of money. He even found her clients, gave her advice on how to petition potential subscribers, and solicited the funds she needed to pay the debts for which she was imprisoned and to establish herself as a shopkeeper. The letter he wrote to her after her return to Ireland is full of the good-natured praise and advice of a loving father. Cibber was perhaps the best of all Laetitia's fathers, for, as the tone of the letter suggests, his recognition of her shortcomings did not inhibit his appreciation of her talents and his sincere delight in her accomplishments. Perhaps in some way Laetitia compensated for Cibber's disappointment in his own daughter, the actress Charlotte Charke.

Father figures aside, the single most important man in Mrs. Pilkington's life was, of course, her husband. If her version of their relationship is incoherent in places, it is a reflection of the chaotic life she was forced to lead as a result of the dissolution of the marriage. Her attempt to exonerate herself of all blame for the marital breakdown includes a denial that she married against her parents' wishes. In the early eighteenth century, it had become commonplace for young people to choose their own spouses. But the right of parental veto was strongly entrenched, and in cases where parental consent was not even sought, a wife could expect no support or sympathy if the marriage was in any way unsuccessful. "I have been accused of Disobedience to my Parents," Laetitia tells us, "in marrying without their Consent or Knowledge" (1: 23). Her account of the events leading up to the marriage is somewhat improbable and not very coherent. She insists that her parents' public disapproval of the match had little to do with their true feelings, and that they in fact privately encouraged her to marry Matthew as soon as possible. Indeed, as we have already seen, Mrs. Pilkington accuses her mother of putting her in the way of falling in love with Matthew by eliminating all her other suitors. Clearly, she wants to be seen as having had no part in the decision that led to her destruction.

After their marriage, Matthew moved into the Van Lewen home with all his worldly possessions: a harpsichord, an owl, and a cat. When Matthew proved unable to get along with Laetitia's parents, the young parson's father bought him a tiny house, where Laetitia gave birth to her four children, one of whom died shortly before the marriage dissolved. All went well in the early years, but Matthew, who was having difficulty getting his own poetry published, became jealous of the praise his young poetical wife was receiving from all sides:

Mr. P——n viewed me with scornful, yet with jealous Eyes. And tho' I never presumed to vye with him for Pre-eminence, well knowing he not only surpassed me in natural Talents, but also had the Advantage of having those Talents improved by Learning; and was sensible the Compliments I received were rather paid to me as a Woman, in whom any thing a Degree above Ignorance appears surprizing, than to any Merit I really possessed; he thought proper to insult me every Moment. Indeed he did not beat me, which some of the good-natured Ladies have brought as an Argument that he was an excellent Husband.

(1: 119)

It is not difficult to understand her bitterness and disappointment. Her knowledge that the praise of her talent is conditional precludes any sense of satisfaction she might otherwise find in it—a sense of satisfaction that could have compensated for the pain of Matthew's jealousy. She must be grateful not only for conditional praise but also for small mercies: at least the continual abuse she has to endure is verbal and not physical.

Swift used his influence to secure Matthew a one-year appointment as chaplain to Alderman Barber, who was on his way to England to serve as Lord Mayor of London for a year. "I was very desirous of going with him," writes Laetitia, "but he told me plainly he did not want such an Incumbrance as a Wife, and that he did not intend to pass there for a married Man; and that in short he could not taste any Pleasure where I was" (1: 123). When he arrived at London, instead of taking quarters in the vicinity of the Lord Mayor's house, Matthew chose an apartment in the more exciting theater district[28] and became involved in an affair with the actress Mrs. Heron.

Animosity between Laetitia and Matthew eased somewhat during the first nine months of his stay in London. They exchanged some tender letters, in one of which Matthew declared "that he heartily wished [Laetitia] in *London*" (1: 153). She responded by booking passage to England. Coincidentally, Alderman Barber's wife, who was also a young poetical protégée of Swift, was on the same ship; Mrs. Barber's mission was to become clear to Laetitia much later. Laetitia was met cheerfully enough by her husband, who was accompanied by James Worsdale. At Matthew's insistence, Laetitia spent her first evening in London in Worsdale's company with a tacit recommendation from her husband to accept his friend as a lover:

So, it seems, I was to be the Bait, wherewith he was to angle for Gold out of a Rival's Pocket: A Scheme which had a twofold Prospect of Gain annexed to it; for a while a Lover has Hope, he seldom quits the Chace; and will even thank the Husband, for taking the friendly Freedom of using his Purse; and yet should the Gallant be detected in taking any friendly Freedoms with the Wife in return, the Law is all against him, Damages and Imprisonment must ensue.

(1: 158)

As for Matthew's plans for the first evening of his wife's visit, he had a previous commitment: a theater engagement, followed by a rendezvous with Mrs. Heron. Matthew continued to throw Laetitia and Worsdale together, but Laetitia soon convinced him she had no intention of yielding.

When Matthew's appointment expired he refused to return to Ireland. The part of Mrs. Pilkington's narrative that deals with Matthew's behavior in London after she returned home has been considerably fleshed out by Iris Barry. According to her, Alderman Barber was "inclined to criticize [Matthew's] staying in London without his wife when his year's chaplaincy was over. That Matthew had not been very assiduous in his attendances worried him far less than that he had been extravagant."[29] Lord Bolingbroke wrote to Swift describing Matthew as a person "who wants morals, and as I hear, decency sometimes."[30]

But Matthew's romantic liaisons, his inattention to professional duties, and his treatment of his wife were the least of his London misadventures. Swift learned to regret his sponsorship of Matthew, but Swift himself was the cause of part of the disgrace under which the young clergyman returned to Dublin. Up to the time of Matthew's arrival in London, Swift had been sending his highly political and treasonous poetry to Pope, who got it published in the same *Miscellany* that printed his own libelous work. Swift thought Pope was getting too much of the credit for these "anonymous" satires, so he engaged Matthew to find a publisher for his manuscripts. He also allowed Matthew to pocket the proceeds. No doubt Matthew received the best possible price for Swift's "Life and Character of Dean Swift" by telling the publisher who actually wrote it. Swift did not discover until two years later that Matthew had betrayed him in this instance. In the meantime he continued to use Matthew as a cat's-paw. Sometime during the early days of Laetitia's visit, Mrs. Barber paid a call on Matthew and delivered a package to him. Laetitia had no reason to be suspicious of this visit from the wife of Matthew's employer. It was not until after she returned to Ireland that the meaning behind the visit became clear to her. Apparently the package was from Swift and contained his treasonous satire, "An Epistle to a Lady." Shortly after Matthew had it published anonymously, the authorities moved in and arrested the publisher, the printer, Matthew, and Mrs. Barber. It apparently did not take much to get Matthew to confess the name of the real author.[31]

Matthew's subsequent imprisonment went hard with Laetitia at home. She was examined and cross-examined on her husband's behalf. There was also no money coming in from Matthew with which to pay the household expenses.

Finally, Matthew was released, and he wrote to Laetitia telling her that he wanted to come home but had no money. After much cajoling she obtained twenty pounds from her father and Matthew was brought back to Dublin. He was pale and ill, and Laetitia nursed him back to health at the expense of her own. Finally, her father sent her off to Cork to recover at the home of his brother. On her return she learned that Matthew had quarreled so violently with her father that he had disowned both of them. Laetitia did not see her father again until a few days before he died.

Shortly after her father's death, Laetitia's youngest child died and Matthew embarked upon an affair with the Widow Warren. At one point he left for several weeks, leaving no money and locking the garden and the larder so that his wife and children had to rely on the charity of Matthew's father and others. When Matthew returned he tried again to arrange for Laetitia's seduction by one of his friends, for he was determined to be rid of her. During the weeks after his return from the Widow Warren, Matthew forced Laetitia into sex, insulted her continually, and beat their children.

On the night Matthew threw his wife out of the house she was entertaining a gentleman in her bedroom. Here is Laetitia's account of the incident:

> I own myself very indiscreet in permitting any Man to be at an unseasonable Hour in my Bed-Chamber; but Lovers of Learning will, I am sure, pardon me, as I solemnly declare, it was the attractive Charms of a new Book, which the Gentleman would not lend me, but consented to stay till I read it through, that was the sole Motive of my detaining him. But the Servants, being bribed by their Master, let in twelve Watchmen at the Kitchen Window, who, though they might have opened the Chamber-Door, chose rather to break it to pieces, and took the Gentleman and myself Prisoners.
>
> (1: 230)

So incredible is this story that it is hardly surprising Mrs. Pilkington's critics find it difficult to take her seriously. However, Spacks's analysis of the incident is instructive in that it helps us to identify Mrs. Pilkington's need to make her life fit some coherent, overall pattern: "In her interpretation of [the] facts, she chooses to emphasize her devotion to learning as an emblem of her hopeless lot. . . . Mrs. Pilkington's specific example of her own betrayal by reading—the man in her bedchamber while she engrosses herself in his book—is less than convincing, but the example, invented or distorted though it may be, epitomizes her repeated experience of finding her gifts turning always to her disadvantage."[32] The same "love of learning" that earned her nothing but empty praise and Matthew's insults at the beginning of their marriage now puts an end to it.

The *Dublin Evening Post* published news of the sentence of divorce for adultery, and Swift wrote to Alderman Barber that Matthew had "proved the falsest rogue, and [Laetitia] the most profligate whore in either kingdom."[33] Laetitia was spurned by women and sexually harassed by men. She legally appealed for and was awarded financial support from Matthew but he defaulted. Finally, Worsdale arrived from London, and, upon learning what had transpired, visited Laetitia and gave her her first ghostwriting assignment. Before she left for London, she gave birth to a daughter whom Matthew refused to recognize. Laetitia was unwilling to leave the child "upon the parish," as Matthew suggested, but does not say with whom she left it when she departed. Several years later she got news that it had died.

She received reports of Matthew from time to time—most of them bad. She claims Matthew tried to sell her children into slavery and that he was only stopped through her intervention (she wrote the authorities in Dublin). She also claims to have received news that he beat the children regularly. Whether or not Matthew treated his children as cruelly as Laetitia claims, his will suggests that he was entirely capable of it:

> "Item. To my son William Pilkington, who never felt a filial affection for me (to the utmost of my observation) I give the sum of five pounds sterlg and to those two abandond wretches John Carteret Pilkington and Elizabeth Pilkington I give the sum of one Shilling if Demanded within 12 months, and I should abhorr to mention them in any Deed of mine, if it were not to prevent all possibility of Dispute or litigation."[34]

Whatever one thinks of Mrs. Pilkington's version of the facts, it is clear that Matthew remained true to the end to the character she gave him. Iris Barry calls Laetitia "a silly little thing to protest so much and fight so ardently to keep up appearance," and yet Laetitia had nothing more to lose by doing so and everything to win if she succeeded in vindicating her "Innocence." That women who forfeit their so-called innocence also lose their credibility is a fact of life that is not unique to the eighteenth century, and herein lies the timelessness of her story. Traditionally, the "honest" woman is the sexually virtuous one, the implication being—as rape cases in twentieth-century law courts continue to demonstrate—that the "unchaste" woman is dishonest and therefore not to be believed.

For women in eighteenth-century England, a move out of the respectable roles of daughter, wife, and mother was almost certainly a move into "unrespectable" ones. For example, the "virtue" of actresses and women writers was always highly suspect, and in fact these professions were often regarded as synonymous with prostitution. Even domestics, shop girls, and milliners' apprentices, as a cursory look at the fiction and periodical literature of the age will reveal, were considered fair game for licentious men-about-town. Women without position, money, or skills, who were forced into the tougher world outside the domestic sphere, had few acceptable role models upon whom to pattern a new identity independent of the men who raised or married them. Mrs. Pilkington sought role models and found only two:

> . . . amongst the Ladies who have taken up the Pen, I never met with but two who deserved the Name of a *Writer;* the first is Madam *Dacier,* whose Learning Mr. *Pope,* while he is indebted to her for all the Notes on *Homer,* endeavours to depreciate; the second is Mrs. *Catherine Philips,* the matchless *Orinda,* celebrated by Mr. *Cowly,* Lord *Orrery,* and all the Men of Genius who lived in her Time.

> (2: 294).

On the whole, however, she was not encouraged by her sister poets, for "the wicked Art of painting up Vice in attractive Colours" was practiced, she believed, by "too many of our Female Writers, . . . to the Destruction of Thousands, amongst whom Mrs. *Manly* and Mrs. *Haywood* deserve the foremost Rank" (2: 293). Given this depressing situation, it is not surprising that what Laetitia Pilkington's *Memoirs* document is a process of self-creation.

Our literary history is characterized by the absence of language and literary forms that adequately express female reality. Eighteenth-century society allowed women to be either virtuous or infamous but the realities of female life seldom fit either of these two categories: Mrs. Pilkington felt that the latter category did not describe her, so for her self-creation she chose the former. There were no other options. And in choosing the former she had to rely on fictional conventions, for only in fiction can the truly "virtuous" woman exist. In shaping her memoir like a romance, Mrs. Pilkington subverts both memoir and romance forms in order to compensate for the inadequacies of both.

The subversion of inappropriate language and literary forms in order to communicate female experience is now a widely recognized phenomenon in women's writing. In addition to the creation of new forms through the fusion of traditional ones, two of the most common literary devices that characterize this phenomenon are characters who function as doubles representing alternatives to the heroine's experience, and images of entrapment and enclosure which express the narrowness of women's lives.[35] These two devices characterize the second and third volume of Mrs. Pilkington's *Memoirs,* the volumes which relate her nine-year adventure in London. Volume one also contains at least two important passages which prefigure the proliferation of doubles and traps in volumes two and three. It is perhaps best to examine these passages as they appear chronologically in the text, in order to get a sense of their escalating intensity—an intensity that reflects Mrs. Pilkington's increasing desperation to reach some kind of conclusion about herself before time and publication space run out for her.

The fragmentary nature of female domestic life with its constant interruptions trains women in the art of fitting tasks into short spans of time. Not only as a woman, but also as a poet, Mrs. Pilkington is used to working within relatively short, self-contained units, and many of the most self-revealing passages in the *Memoirs* are isolated "stories" or anecdotes that are seemingly disconnected from the rest of the narrative. Each of these passages is shaped like a tiny short story in which a plot develops to a climax followed by a resolution. These passages often feature characters who are appearing for the first time in the narrative and who never appear again. The story of Sir John Meade, which we have already examined, is the first example of this kind of passage. Mrs. Pilkington rummages through her store of ancestors in search of someone who can tell her something about herself, and Sir John is the only one of her many ancestors who merits a story of his own—a kind of "mini-memoir" that reflects aspects of Laetitia's own story or the story she would like to write. The proud and clever Irishman's triumph over the even prouder Englishman is a kind of unfulfilled fantasy for Laetitia whose pride and wit are severely tested—indeed, all but overcome—by the alien and hostile atmosphere of London.

Others of these passages are merely tiny character sketches of vignettes containing some element of mystery or magic. A case in point concerns the young woman who comes to study midwifery with Laetitia's father when Laetitia is in her early teens. The daughter of a poor, illiterate country couple, this eighteen-year-old girl is the "Mistress of *Hebrew, Greek, Latin* and *French,* and [understands] the *Mathematicks,* as well as most Men" (1: 27). Given her humble background, "her Learning appear[s] like the Gift poured out on the Apostles, of speaking all Languages, without the Pains of Study; or like the intuitive Knowledge of Angels." Despite the fact that she remains closely associated with the Van Lewen household for at least two years and becomes Laetitia's constant companion, Laetitia can never get a satisfactory explanation as to how this "female Philosopher" became so learned; "only she said, 'she had received some little Instruction from the Minister of the Parish, when she could spare Time from her Needlework, to which she was closely kept by her Mother' " (1: 28). This mysterious woman, whose "Piety [is] not inferior to her Learning," also writes "elegantly both in Verse and Prose"; however, "Whether it was owing to her own Desire, or the Envy of those who survived her, I know not; but for her various and beautiful Writings, except one Poem of her's in Mrs. *Barber's* Works, I have never seen any published; 'tis true, as her Turn was chiefly to philosophical or divine subjects, they might not be agreeable to the present taste" (1: 28–29). Mrs. Pilkington includes two of this woman's poems in her *Memoirs,* one of which, "To Miss Laetitia Van Lewen," is signed "Constantia." Constantia is Laetitia's double: she both is and is not Laetitia.[36] Clearly there are parallels in her story with Laetitia's own: the triumph of intellectual achievement over considerable maternal pressure to cultivate only the "feminine" skills; the publication of only one of her many poems (Laetitia sells her "Trial of Constancy" to a newspaper shortly after she arrives in London but never manages to publish the collection for which she solicits subscriptions). Constantia also represents the "unlived life": the languages Laetitia never learns; the piety she never cultivates; the vocational skills she never acquires. Constantia also has a close association with Dr. Van Lewen—a point which becomes more significant when we learn of Laetitia's estrangement from her beloved father. Only through external sources do we discover the identity of this mysterious woman: she is Mrs. Grierson, another protégée of Jonathan Swift. True, Mrs. Grierson's name does appear—much later—in Mrs. Pilkington's narrative, but she never connects it with her father's young apprentice.

Another of these short, self-contained anecdotes reads like an episode from *Pamela*. It concerns an incident which occurs during Laetitia's visit with Matthew in London. Matthew obliges Laetitia to make a trip to Windsor with Worsdale. She expects it will be a one-day return journey but soon discovers that Worsdale's plan is to remain overnight. They check in at a large, noisy inn, and Laetitia is so nervous and apprehensive that she starts at every sound. When she feigns weariness and asks the maid to show her to her chamber, she discovers to her horror that only one room containing one bed has, on Worsdale's instructions, been provided for the two of them: "I was now in a manner convinced, there was Treachery intended against me, and reproached my desiring Swain in such bitter Terms, that he had no Way to prove his Innocence, but by retiring, tho' very reluctantly, to another Apartment; and I took special Care to barricade my own, not only double-locking it, but also placing all the Chairs and Tables against the Door to prevent a Possibility of being surprized" (1: 164). This triumph over the lecherous Worsdale has a hollow ring to it, for it is dependent upon her self-imprisonment—a confinement of double locks and barricades that are symbolic of the social conventions that entrap her.

Mrs. Pilkington rises very early next morning in order to do some sight-seeing. She sees nothing worth mentioning but Windsor castle, "the Palace of the *Edwards* and the *Henrys*," which touches her "with something like a religious Veneration" (1: 165). The castle looms symbolically over this story like a shrine sacred to ancient patriarchal authority, and her veneration of it springs from the same instinctive source as her fear of Worsdale in his assault upon the citadel of her virtue. In the spirit of Pamela's Mr. B———, Worsdale now attends her "with great Respect" but "tenderly reproache[s]" her for her "Cruelty" of the previous evening. He gives her "no farther Cause of Displeasure" and brings her safely back to London.

Mrs. Pilkington ends this story with a literary device common to novels of the period: an authorial intrusion in which the narrator addresses the reader directly: "But pray, gentle Reader, suppose it had happened otherwise; that Night[,] Solitude, an agreeable and importunate Lover, should have prevailed on human, yielding Frailty, whom could my Husband so properly have blamed for it as himself? He who best knew our Frames, bids us avoid Temptation, as the surest Method, nay and perhaps the only one of avoiding Sin; for who so firm that may not be seduced?" (1: 165). Does all this speculation in the form of conditional verbs amount to a covert admission of guilt? Is she asking her "gentle Reader" to have mercy on her "human, yielding Frailty" prevailed upon by "an agreeable and importunate Lover"? It is conceivable that this passage is Mrs. Pilkington's way of striking a compromise between her own experience and the version she feels constrained to offer her readers.

In the spirit of Pamela she gives in to Worsdale's point of view:

> . . . to have mentioned Mr. W———le's Attempt [to Matthew], why, to say the Truth, I looked upon it as a Thing which any Man in the same Circumstances might naturally be guilty of, even tho' he had no previous liking to, or Thought of the Woman. So, as there was no Harm done, I judged it most prudent to be silent. Besides, no Faults are so easily pardoned by our Sex, as those we believe to be occasioned by our own Charms, the eager Lover's constant Excuse, and which our Vanity is but too apt to admit as a reasonable one.
>
> (1: 166–67)

Characteristically, the oppressor's "Faults" are easily "pardoned" while the blame shifts to the victim whose "Charms" and "Vanity" are the cause of women's undoing. Laetitia is caught in that familiar and powerful trap which has throughout patriarchal history kept women in the confined space allotted to them. But the moment these words are on the page she realizes that she has written herself into a trap and like a caged creature she lashes out in impotent rage:

> Of all Things in Nature, I most wonder why Men should be severe in their Censures on our Sex, for a Failure in Point of Chastity: Is it not monstrous, that our Seducers should be our Accusers? Will they not employ Fraud, nay, often Force to gain us? What various Arts, what Stratagems, what Wiles will they use for our Destruction? but that once accomplished, every opprobrious Term with which our Language so plentifully abounds, shall be bestowed on us, even by the very Villains who have wronged us.
>
> (1: 167)

The suggestion that men use language as a weapon against women is significant here, for the *Memoirs* are an attempt to appropriate the male weapon of the written word and turn it back upon the "Villains who have wronged" Laetitia.

In keeping with this reversal is the subtle implication, in the tone of outrage and exasperation, that it is men (not necessarily just women) who exhibit irrationality, inconsistency, and unfairness in their dealings with the opposite sex. Indeed, men have it both ways: they have the pleasure of seducing women into "immoral" behavior and the added satisfaction of accusing them of immorality.

The enormousness of urban space, with its promise of freedom and anonymity, is not the London Mrs. Pilkington introduces us to in volume two. Her conditioning as a "harmless houshold Dove," whose natural habitat is the narrowness of domestic space, coupled with her chronic poverty and her reputation for infamy which reaches London before she does, denies her the freedom and anonymity she might have expected. She takes expensive rooms across from White's Chocolate House,[37] an establishment that turns out to be a ready market for her poems, and, probably, her charms. She is financially supported by an old Colonel to whom she writes love letters which he boastfully exhibits to his friends at White's. Colley Cibber pays his first visit, and between his generosity and that of the other lords and lesser gentlemen who pass in and out of her rooms, she manages comfortably, except in the summers when Parliament adjourns and the gentlemen leave town for their country estates. Then she must find other, less expensive quarters until the new session of Parliament opens, when she can return to her rooms near White's. It is during one of these earliest summers that she boards and rooms in a "very genteel House in *Greenstreet, Grosvenor-Square*" (a suburban area during the eighteenth century), where the landlord is "Valet de Chambre to the Earl of *Stair*, and his Wife a top Laundress" (2: 96). It is here that she becomes acquainted with a mysterious new lodger whose story is another isolated anecdote that unfolds like a plot in a novel. The inclusion of her story in the *Memoirs* and its relationship to an excluded incident in Mrs. Pilkington's life help to demonstrate the truth of Virginia Woolf's conclusion about her—namely that "it is her duty to entertain; it is her instinct to conceal."

Pilkington knows nothing about this "very genteel pretty Woman," for the landlady, noting that her new lodger brought "very good Furniture" with her, does not think it necessary to make further inquiries. The woman, whose name we learn much later, and only indirectly, is pregnant, and for two months she locks herself in her room and receives no visitors. Finally, at two o'clock one morning, a man, who the woman claims is her husband, comes to visit her and leaves again early in the morning. He comes in the same manner several more times, and to Laetitia these nocturnal visits appear "rather to wear the Face of an Amour, than lawful Matrimony" (2: 101). The visits suddenly end as mysteriously as they began, and during the ensuing weeks, Laetitia, who has managed to establish an intimacy with the woman, often catches her in tears. One day, Laetitia asks her to tell her story and the woman promises her that if she "would be her Bedfellow that Night, she [will] relate . . . her unhappy Story" (2: 103).

"Wished for Night" comes, and the woman begins her long tale about how she became the victim of bigamy. Her poor but honest parents, the early death of her mother, her marriage to Mr. H———l, their four children (none of whom lived above a few days), her husband's desertion, her undying love for Mr. H———l despite his bigamy—all these details are skillfully calculated to inspire our sympathy and outrage, and are spun out at length in a most engaging and suspense-filled style. Midway in Mrs. H———l's narrative she and Laetitia both burst into tears and Mrs. H———l falls asleep sobbing in Laetitia's arms. Laetitia "long[s] as much for the next Night, as the *Sultan,* in *The Arabian Nights Entertainment,* did to hear the charming *Scherazade's* fine stories" (2: 108). Night finally comes, and Mrs. H———l picks up her narrative. Her husband had been thrown into prison awaiting trial for bigamy. She was the only person in a position to testify against him, and he had talked her out of it. Until his visits to her ceased a few weeks ago she had been kept by her husband as a mistress. Now she has no money and there will soon be a child . . . what, she asks Laetitia, should she do? Laetitia promptly visits the bigamist:

> . . . with a marvellous Assurance, he said, he could not give Charity to every Body; that he had often assisted that unfortunate Person; that she ought to work for her Bread, as many of her Betters did, and a Number of such inhuman Speeches, common on those Occasions. I told him her present Conditions did not enable her to perform any but Needle-work, and that he who put her into it should support her. . . . He bade me explain myself; I told him, he perfectly understood me, and therefore it was not necessary; but that if he pleased, I would tell Mrs. *H———l* the second, of his Midnight visits to his Wife. . . . putting a Couple of Guineas into my Hand, [he] said aloud, Madam, I shall take care, and mind your Directions. . . .
>
> (2: 112–13)

This is Laetitia's first recorded experience as a blackmailer; it is a skill she will use many more times, but on her own behalf. Mrs. H———l and her baby die in childbirth and Laetitia can only hope that the prison this bigamist once escaped will someday be his permanent residence.

This episode is interesting not only because it demonstrates Mrs. Pilkington's considerable skill in narrative technique, both in Mrs. H———l's story and in the frame in which the story is set, but also because it features Mrs. Pilkington as a compassionate and heroic friend. It also shows her triumph over a man who is perhaps even more villainous than Matthew. The parallels between Mrs. Pilkington's and Mrs. H——l's life stories are obvious. Less obvious is the possibility that this story is a replacement for one which Mrs. Pilkington chose not to tell in her *Memoirs:* the story of her daughter Elizabeth.

Samuel Richardson's correspondence contains a letter from Mrs. Pilkington, dated December, 1745, in which she begs him for money: "My daughter is come to me big with child, naked and desolate; and because I would not let her lye in the street, my saint-like methodist landlady has padlocked the door, and turned us both there. My own writings she has secured, as well as a few small matters, she, my child, had provided for her child. I have less authority to blame her than perhaps another mother would take."[38] A few days later she writes to him again, begging that his wife spare her "a little old linen of any kind," because she and her daughter, who do not even have proper lodgings, also have nothing in which to wrap the expected baby.[39] All the *Memoirs* tell us of Elizabeth's arrival in London is that she came in financial need, saw that she could expect no help from her mother, and went out to work as a lady's maid. Nothing about her pregnancy is mentioned. Perhaps Mrs. H——l's story, in which Laetitia plays the role of supportive mother, in some way compensates for Elizabeth's story—a story which, for the protection of both her own reputation and that of her daughter, is better left untold.

The story of Mrs. H——l is not the only incident in the *Memoirs* that ends in sudden death. Directly after the death of her companion, Mrs. Pilkington becomes acquainted with the owners of a bookshop who invite her to spend an evening with them at cards. She meets at the card table a promising new friend, an admiral's son and a Member of Parliament called Mr. Rooke, who impresses Mrs. Pilkington, first, because he admires her poetry, and second, because he praises his wife for her "unmatched Wit and Beauty":

> I told him, I was glad to find one Person of Distinction, who was not ashamed to do Justice to the Merits of his Lady: "I should be a Scoundrel, said he to refuse it; she gave me the Preference to a Man of a much larger Fortune, to whom her Friends had destined her; an Obligation never to be forgot by a grateful Spirit." This Gentleman had such an uncommon generous way of thinking, that, instead of minding the Game, I was quite attentive to him, which he observing, said, "Take away the Cards, they are only fit to amuse such as are incapable of tasting a more rational Entertainment."
>
> (2: 116)

He prefers not only good conversation but also tea, as opposed to stronger drink. High on this "Chat-inspiring liquor," he and Laetitia discover their mutual interest in politics and good fun, and they spend the evening exchanging ribald political anecdotes. Mr. Rooke asks to see her the next day, and when Laetitia asks him to fix the hour he gives her a recital of his daily schedule ending with bed at midnight. She suggests he come to her in the hour he usually spends in a coffeehouse but, he asks,

> " . . . what think you of the last Hour, wherein I go to Bed" "Oh, Sir, you are so much better engaged, it would not only be Wickedness, but Folly also, to think of that at all."
>
> Well, depend on it, said he, I'll see you tomorrow; so we took Leave for ever, for the very first News I heard next Morning, was, that Mr. *Rooke*, a little while after he arose, fell down in an Apoplectic Fit, and instantly expired.
>
> (2: 128–29)

This story is interesting because it features a Mrs. Pilkington who conforms to neither the virtuous nor the infamous female stereotype. She is a person whose talent and intellect are appreciated by a man who not only respects women but also thinks it not beneath him to discuss politics with them. Their naughty stories reveal them both as liberated but not indecent, and his suggestion that they sleep together is made lightly enough to be a joke but nevertheless suggests that Laetitia is sexually as well as intellectually attractive. Mr. Rooke's sudden death, like that of Mrs. H——l, is like the bursting of a fantasy bubble, and Laetitia is left to ponder Dr. Delany's mirror poem:

> I found, by these two melancholy Events, there was nothing serious in Mortality; all was but Toys! I frequently recollected Dr. *Delany's* beautiful Lines on seeing himself in the Glass:
> *When I resolve this evanescent State*
> *Of short Duration, and uncertain Date;*
> *My Being, and my Stay dependent still,*
> *Not on my own, but on another's Will;*
> *I ask myself, as I my Form review,*
> *Which is the real Shadow of the two?*
>
> (2: 129)

The fact that these two stories recall this poem to Laetitia's mind is significant. Like Delany's mirror, these two stories—whatever their relationship to real events—reflect aspects of Laetitia which, like Delany's reflection, are both "real" and a "Shadow" to their author.

If Mrs. Pilkington fantasizes about ideal friendships with ideal men it is entirely understandable, for arriving in London in the wake of her own scandal she had no opportunity to establish relationships on her own terms. Although Iris Barry thinks Laetitia silly to "fight so ardently to keep up appearance," it is clear that what she is fighting for is something that men take for granted:

the power to create herself. Furthermore, some of her best writing occurs when she is fighting hardest. For example, although she has adopted the name of Meade from her illustrious ancestors, she is hounded by the reputation of Mrs. Pilkington, the adulterous Irishwoman:

> . . . my Name was *Meade*, for by that I always went in *London;* so that the numerous Stories of Mrs. P——n's being in Taverns, Bagnio's, etc. which my Husband says he can prove, *(Mem.* he lyes) never appertained to me; but to his own C——sin N——y P——n, whose Father lives in *Pill-Lane,*—and who is herself as common a Prostitute as ever traversed the Hundreds of *Drury.*
>
> (2: 126)

She attempts to dissociate herself from this questionable profession by demonstrating her contempt for it. Some of her descriptions of prostitutes are hilarious. For example, she takes quarters above a milliner's shop which (to her surprise, of course) turns out to be a front for a "house of civil Reception"; here is a description of the "landlady." Mrs. Smith:

> . . . Woman is a Term too gentle for her, who had not even Decency to hide her Shame.
> To give my Reader a Taste of her Cleanliness: She told me herself she had not combed her Head for three Years, which, I believe, was true, because she was not Mistress of a Comb, except when she made free with mine, than which nothing could be more offensive to me, so that her Hair, tho' naturally fine, being quite matted on a filthy Hair-cap, seemed to be a Composition of raw Silk and Moss, such as I remember to have stolen a Lock of from the Head of Good Duke *Humphrey,* at *St. Albans,* three hundred Years after his Death.
>
> (2: 143–44)

Mrs. Smith is rivalled only by her colleague, Mrs. Cunningham, so-called because it is the name of the man who "ruined" her:

> . . . her Chin, which had on it a comely black Beard, almost met her Nose, there not being a Tooth in the Way to bar their Union. I am sure, had *Don Quixote* seen her, he would have endeavoured to disenchant her Mustachio's. Her Eyes were black and fierce, her Back nobly prominent, her Dress tawdry, and take her for all in all, I hope I never shall look upon her Like again. I was doubtful whether it was not a Man in Woman's Clothes; but it if were a Creature of the Feminine Gender, I concluded it must be a Witch. . . .
>
> (2: 166)

Descriptions of prostitutes in masculine terms may be an eighteenth-century literary convention;[40] however, the degree to which Mrs. Pilkington exploits that convention is significant. By calling both these women's gender so clearly into question she reveals her own belief in prostitution as a betrayal of femininity. But her protestations of contempt are over-strong and thus do not ring quite true. As a result she raises suspicions in her readers about her own association with the profession of prostitution. By denying so strongly any association with these women—even to the point of questioning the femininity they have in common with her—she succeeds only in identifying herself with them. Indeed, the prostitutes she describes seem to function as doubles representing aspects of her London career which she would rather not think of in infamous terms.

Mrs. Cunningham and Mrs. Smith are brought to mind by a curious story that Mrs. Pilkington tells in an attempt to explain why a certain Lord D——le has spread scandalous stories about her. She claims that shortly after her arrival in London, his Lordship, titillated by the scandal associated with her, hires a woman to arrange a rendezvous for him. She tells this odious messenger that she does not know his Lordship and therefore declines the invitation:

> But the *Harridan*, being resolved not to lose her Reward, told my L——
> —d I would meet him somewhere, indeed I do not know the Place, and
> introduced to him a great, lusty, masculine Woman, dressed in a Cali-
> manco Cap and Cloak, or long Riding-hood. I believe his L——d——p
> wondered that such a Creature had made any Noise in the World; so tell-
> ing her, he was sorry he had given her the Trouble of coming there, he
> gave her a Guinea, and hastily departed.
>
> (2: 278)

Whatever Laetitia intends us to think of her double it is clear she has scored a triumph on Laetitia's behalf—first, by disappointing the gentleman and then by receiving money for services she is not obliged to render. In short, the large and repulsively masculine double gets away with what the diminutive and attractive Laetitia cannot.

As the years go by Mrs. Pilkington finds it increasingly difficult to raise money. She spends much of her time peddling her panegyrics on rich gentlemen, soliciting subscriptions door-to-door, and trying—often unsuccessfully—to beg money from clergymen and other officials reputed to be charitable. At one point, when she has been three days without food, she determines to end her life. The story of her two aborted attempts at suicide is interesting not only because of its relationship to the themes of doubles and traps, but also in terms of the dramatic embellishments Mrs. Pilkington employs in telling the story. She spins out the details at length in somber language that evokes a sense of mystery and suspense.

On the evening of her third day of hunger, she enters St. James's Park and seats herself by Rosamond's Pond: "the Moon, apparent Queen, unveiled her peerless Light," she recalls, "and I waited in the silent Shade, resolved to execute my dreadful Purpose, as soon as I could do it without Observation" (2: 209). But a young woman and (presumably) her mother sit down beside her. Despite her unresponsiveness they persist in their attempts to engage her in conversation. They finally succeed—so well in fact that they suddenly realize it has grown late and that the gates of the park have been locked for the night. However, the garden surrounding the home of these two well-dressed and genteel ladies opens onto the park and they invite Laetitia to come through and stop for supper with them:

> We were let in at a Back-door, by a Servant in Livery, to a very genteel House, where, on a Sopha, sat a very handsome Man in a Gold Brocade Night-Gown, to whom the young Lady presented me, and said, he was her Spouse; the Cloth was ready laid, and a cold Supper on the Table: I would very fain have prevailed on the Lady to permit me to go through her House home, for I could easily perceive the Gentleman's Civility was quite forced, and, that he was impatient to revenge on his Wife the Liberty she had taken of inviting a Stranger in; which indeed, I believe, she did on no other Account, but, that she thought Decency would prevent him from giving her a Beating, of which, it seems, he was very liberal, though he was but a Footman when the Lady married him, and threw herself, and twenty thousand Pounds away upon him, as I afterwards learned.
>
> (2: 210)

In spite of her three days of hunger Laetitia can hardly swallow a bite in this house, for the tense atmosphere, she tells us, recalls "the Fear and Terror I always felt in Mr. P——n's, to which, if my Father, Mother, or any Friend came, it threw me into Agonies, being well assured, they would never depart without receiving some gross Affront . . . " (2: 211).

The themes of this story are by now familiar: the entrapment in the park, the entrapment of the unnamed woman—Mrs. Pilkington's double—in a disastrous marriage to a man beneath her in status and of her own choosing. Significantly, although they temporarily frustrate Mrs. Pilkington's plans, and do indeed offer her a route by which to escape her entrapment in the park, the two women cannot show her the route by which she may escape the mental trap she is in. For the next evening she finds herself back in the same spot in the park. This time she gets as far as making several abortive attempts to throw herself into the pond. Suddenly a man approaches and asks: "Lord, can this be Mrs. *Pilkington?*" Laetitia senses that he has guessed her purpose, for although she begs to be left alone he insists on taking her to the Royal Vineyard nearby. She discovers that he is Captain Hamilton, who has met her once at the home of her uncle in Cork. Over dinner and champagne she tells him her whole sad story, culminating in her suicide attempt. "After we had regaled ourselves," she writes, "we left the *Park*, and he was so kind to see me to my Lodging; where, putting a couple of Guineas into my Hand, we parted, and he promised to see me next Morning; but I saw him no more" (2: 216).

The initial suicide attempt and its "replay" the following day are worth comparing. Both events take place late in the evening, yet on the first evening Laetitia is trapped in the park, while on the following night the gates remain open until after her dinner with Captain Hamilton. This has symbolic significance in terms of the relative powerlessness of her female rescuers as compared to the power of her male liberator. Captain Hamilton achieves what the two women could not: the women fail to inspire Laetitia because, in spite of their access to the material things Laetitia lacks, the only vision of an alternative to suicide they can offer is the bleakness of their own lives. Only the (male) freedom Captain Hamilton represents can release her and cause her, as she tells us, "once more . . . to believe myself under the Favour and Protection of the Almighty" (2: 217). Timeworn fictional conventions are recalled in Captain Hamilton's nick-of-time appearance, and, like the promising Mr. Rooke, he drops as mysteriously and quickly out of Laetitia's life as he dropped into it.

The ultimate entrapment incident in the *Memoirs* is, of course, Mrs. Pilkington's confinement in Marshalsea Prison where she languishes for several weeks for the crime of owing her landlady four shillings. At first she gives in to despair and refuses to eat for three days, but her cell mate forces nourishment on her and she soon recovers her fighting spirit. She applies to a couple of official sources of charity; both send her a guinea—not enough to secure her release but enough to salve the consciences of the donors. One of these donors is a Dr. Mead, a man who "had sixty thousand Pounds left him, to give in such Charities as he thought proper" (2: 194). Mrs. Pilkington had applied to him in person once and received two guineas along with a remarkably rude lecture from the arrogant doctor. Along with the guinea she receives from him in Marshalsea Prison he sends a characteristically rude and arrogant letter. She is determined on revenge, so she relates a story about a fellow prisoner, a woman who claims she is Dr. Mead's wife. Mrs. Pilkington sees her lying drunk in a puddle and asks her cell mate to give her some account of this woman. She learns that the woman had been a servant of the doctor and that she had borne him a child. When at length the doctor parted with his mistress he agreed to pay her five guineas a week, but when he married, the payments began to fall off. She went to his house and caused a scene that exposed him before all his servants:

> Upon this the Doctor stepped into his Chariot, and ordered it to drive to her Lodging, where finding she was indebted to her Landlord, one Mr.

Bradst——t, famous for being a Spy for the D—— of C——, he desired
him to arrest, and put her in Jail. This artful Fellow alledged, it would
be very expensive; but the Doctor having Charity-money enough to supply
such Exigencies, said, he valued not the Expence, so she was secured.
Upon this the poor Wretch was arrested, and thrown into Jail; and from
time to time *Bradst——t* got three hundred Pounds of the Doctor for
keeping her there; till at length the Doctor growing weary of the Expence,
consented to her Releasement; but she had so entirely devoted herself to
drinking, that she died a few Days after she obtained her Liberty.

(2: 225–26)

Whether or not the story is a true one seems immaterial. The fact that she
would tell such a story—true or false—to get revenge demonstrates the intensity of her rage. The coincidence of the woman's assumed name "Mead" and
Laetitia's own adopted name "Meade" makes this poor victim Laetitia's double.
They are also doubles in that they are both betrayed by the father of their
children, both retaliate by exposing their oppressors, and both get thrown into
the Marshalsea for default of rent—a reward for demonstrating an independence of spirit. Like Mrs. H——l and Mr. Rooke, Mrs. Mead also dies, and
thus her story, like theirs, is neatly sealed off from the rest of Mrs. Pilkington's
narrative.

Like the two women who saved Mrs. Pilkington from suicide, her female cell
mate saves her from immediate self-destruction by forcing her to eat. But it
takes a man to release her from prison. Colley Cibber solicits money for her
from no less than sixteen dukes (or so he claims), and Laetitia returns the favor,
not to Cibber but to her fellow inmates, for whom she writes a "pathetic Memorial" which "obtains[s] an Act of Grace for them" (2: 231).

Entrapment is the theme of the story Mrs. Pilkington tells of her overnight
stay in Westminster Abbey. This incident occurs shortly after she goes into the
print-selling business. One evening, in a fit of melancholy over a sad letter
from her son, John, she visits the Abbey and soon finds to her horror that she
has been locked in for the night with the rats and the ghosts of the great. She
wraps herself in the altar rug, falls asleep in the pulpit, and has a kind of
archetypal dream in which the ghosts of various kings and queens of England
enact historical events. Each monarch is featured in a scene depicting his/her
infamy or victimization. These scenes are characterized by Mrs. Pilkington's
unconventional interpretation of history. The most interesting scene depicts
Mary Tudor as a beautiful and learned woman who is forced against her will
into accepting the crown, and who is poisoned to death by her husband, Philip
of Spain. By transforming the infamous "Bloody Mary," the religious fanatic,
into a misunderstood victim, Mrs. Pilkington creates another double for herself
as the victim of a false interpretation of historical events.

Mrs. Pilkington's sense of herself as an unappreciated poet finds expression in the second part of her dream, which features a ghostly procession of great poets. Spenser, "the Prince of Poets in his Time," appears presenting a copy of his epic poem to Queen Elizabeth and receiving from her what looks like a purse of gold: "but the Poet opening it, found nothing in it but Grains, such as they feed the Hogs with, of which he put a large Handful into his Mouth, and instantly dropped down" (2: 266). Significantly, Spenser's reward from the queen is both worthless and fatal. Like Mary Tudor, Spenser is a projection of Mrs. Pilkington herself, for she sees herself as a poet whose rewards include not only worthless praise but also the seeds of her own destruction.

What is most interesting about this Westminster Abbey tale is the fact that it is largely borrowed from "The Apotheosis of Milton," a serialized story by an unidentified author, which opened in the May, 1738, number of the *Gentleman's Magazine*. In that story, the author finds himself locked in Westminster Abbey, falls asleep, and dreams that he is witnessing the arrival in heaven of history's greatest poets. He observes the proceedings of a heavenly assembly composed of Chaucer, Spenser, Shakespeare, and other literary luminaries who entertain petitions for admission from newly arrived poets. It was possibly the following passage from the second installment of the "Apotheosis" that helped fix the story in Mrs. Pilkington's imagination:

> But observe that Lady dressed in the loose *Robe de Chambre* with her Neck and Breasts bare; how much Fire in her Eye! What a passionate Expression in her Motions! And how much Assurance in her Features! Observe what an Indignant Look she bestows on the President, who is telling her, *that none of her Sex has any Right to a Seat there.* How she throws her Eyes about, to see if she can find out any one of the Assembly who inclines to take her Part. No! not one stirs; they who are enclined in her favour are overawed, and the rest shake their Heads; and now she flings out of the Assembly. That extraordinary Woman is *Afra Behn.* . . . [41]

It is not difficult to imagine Mrs. Pilkington as both impressed and depressed by this notion of heaven as a male preserve. "Afra" Behn, like Laetitia, is a victim of gender conventions. Despite his gender, Laetitia's Spenserian double, like Mrs. Behn in this passage, is denied the just rewards of literary talent. But whatever Laetitia's initial reaction to this story, her use of it as an autobiographical vehicle suggests that her sense of herself as a victim extends beyond what the mere facts of her experience can convey.

There are perhaps other, more practical reasons why Mrs. Pilkington resorts to direct borrowing from "The Apotheosis of Milton." The Westminster Abbey incident occurs near the end of her second volume and she is running out of material; volume two is padded out with her unfinished tragedy, "The Roman

Father." This literary winding-down becomes even more obvious in volume three, where the writing begins to break down and the narrative loses coherence. Volume three is written largely in response to public reception of her first two volumes, and that reception, in the form of pamphlets and newspaper items, no doubt made clear to her the futility of any further attempt to reclaim her sullied reputation: "Reputation once gone is never to be retriev'd," she writes in the opening pages of volume three; "The Wise say, it is as often gain'd without Merit, as lost without a Crime; so I must comfort myself the best I can" (3: 4–5). Although she never gives in to the public's perception of her as the infamous whore, she expends far less energy trying to make sense of her past and instead seeks her "comfort" in the destructive power of her pen:

> And here, before I proceed, to give Ease to every Heart, which may possibly suffer any Anxiety, on Account of what might be said of them, I proclaim Peace to all, but those who have directly affronted me. 'Tis but a mean Piece of Cowardice to insult a Woman, and as some Gentlemen have had the Courage to Challenge me, by the known Laws of Chivalry, I have a right to chuse the Weapons; a *Pen* is mine, let them take up another, and may-hap they will meet their Match.
>
> (3: 6)

This shift from creative to destructive literary energy breaks the spell cast by the earlier material. The heroine of the first two volumes is transformed from victim to victimizer as she lashes out vindictively at her critics and various other individuals who have risked the wrath of her pen by either failing in their charity to her or resisting her blackmail.

There are, however, at least two incidents in this final volume which serve as a suitable closure to the story of Mrs. Pilkington's London years. The first of these describes her final encounter with Worsdale. The incident—not surprisingly—is another story of entrapment. After the failure of her printshop, Mrs. Pilkington is forced to seek Worsdale out and once again sell her services as a ghostwriter. Like the goose of golden egg fame, she is kept locked up in Worsdale's rooms where she churns out letters, poems, and even an opera libretto for him. Although she describes this episode as "worse than *Egyptian* Bondage" (3: 47), she is more concerned with entertaining her readers with it than she is with convincing us of the horrors of her imprisonment. For example, here is a description of the meals she shares with Worsdale:

> We had four Play-bills laid for a Table-cloth, Knives, Forks, or Plates, had we none; no matter for that—
> *I had a Blade,*
> *With which my tuneful Pens were made—*

146

> *And, so to make my Dinner sure,*
> *I for a Fork employ'd a Skewer.*

The Butter, when we had any, was deposited in the cool and fragrant Recess of an old Shoe, a Coffee-pot of mine served for as many Uses as ever *Scrub* had, for sometimes it boil'd Coffee, sometimes Tea, it brought small Beer, strong Beer, and I am more than half afraid it has been applied to less noble Uses. . . .

(3: 43–44)

It is in the flash of fanciful moments such as this that we get a sense of some genuine literary talent that both undermines and transcends her attempt to convince us of the "facts."

This talent takes over in the story of her return journey to Ireland. With only two guineas between them, Mrs. Pilkington and her son John set forth on a May morning in a wagon drawn by "Slow-pac'd Cattle . . . adorned with Ribbands and Flowers" (3: 185). She delights in the fine spring weather, the singing of the birds, and "the flower-enamell'd Meads, filled with Cowslips, Primroses, and wild Violets" (3: 186). But no Garden of Eden would be complete without a serpent, and during one of the rest stops they do indeed encounter one: it coils itself around John's leg but soon crawls away without harming him. The encounter with the snake prefigures an incident which occurs the following day. She and John take advantage of a day's stopover at a village inn to explore the surrounding area. They come upon a body hanging from a gallows surrounded by mourners:

One of the Fellows made up to us, and asked where we were going; I told him to our Country, *Ireland*. Arah, said he, are you a Catolic? I said I was! Upon which he said, Faith poor Paddy *Lawler,* who hangs there was a good one. And what, Sir, brought him to so unfortunate an End? Why, said he, he was in Love with a proud scornful Hussey, and she slighted him, so he met her in this Plaish, and because she would not accept of his Shivility, he lent her a Nock on the Head, and so he got his Will of her. She died the next Day, after she had given Information against him; to be sure her Skull was broke, but he did not deshine that.

(3: 188-89)

The rural character and manners of this stranger are perfectly captured in Mrs. Pilkington's rendering of his dialect. His appearance on the scene, as well as the presence of the hanging corpse, like the appearance of the snake, is in startling contrast to the idyllic setting. The casual way in which the man takes for granted a jealous lover's right to do violence to his mistress strikes terror into Laetitia's heart. For fear of inspiring violence against herself, she accepts the man's offer to escort her back to the inn:

When I got to the Inn I told him, I should be glad of his Company, but that I had a jealous Husband, who would certainly kill me, if he found any Man in my Company. Damn the Rogue, said he, if I was you, I would make him a Cuckold in a crack. I desired he would please to accept of a Pot of Drink, which he did, and making a Leg, walk'd off leaving us unmolested, and I blest God I had purchased Life at so cheap a Rate.

(3: 190)

Mrs. Pilkington's lie about her mortal fear of a jealous husband contains a timeless truth that transcends its factual inaccuracy. Although she has blatantly identified herself with the murder victim in this story, the man is totally oblivious to the mortal danger he is inviting her to by advising her to behave like the "proud scornful Hussey" who inspired the jealous Paddy Lawler's wrath. This example of male disregard for the perils of female existence is hardly overstated in this story, for it recalls the fate of characters such as the unfortunate Mrs. H——l and Laetitia's dead prison mate Mrs. Mead.

Mrs. Pilkington's success in escaping unharmed from this incident recalls to her mind a similar incident which occurred during her childhood. She was on a journey with her mother and sister when the coach was held up by a band of highwaymen:

. . . my Mother, with surprizing Presence of Mind, said Gentlemen, you are very welcome to the Coach, my Daughter and I will walk, to oblige you with it; which, Villains, Ruffians, and Murtherers as they were, they would not permit, but only desired we might Huzza for them, this notwithstanding our Terror, we chearfully did; and my Mother said, Gentlemen perhaps you are dry, and gave them a Crown, with which they were so well pleased, that they huzza'd for us, offering to guard us safe to Town; but she alledging that would be too much trouble, they left us with a kind Assurance, that they would drink our Healths, and fight for us any Time we stood in need of their Protection.

(3: 191)

This story is significant because it features as hero Laetitia's mother, who everywhere else in the *Memoirs* is a villain. In fact, it is Laetitia's recollection of this incident which reminds her "That soft Answers turn away Wrath," and by remembering her mother's example years later Laetitia avoids bringing down the wrath of the hanged man's friend upon her. The retelling of this incident not only serves to bring Mrs. Van Lewen into the constellation of doubles that mirror Laetitia's experience but also suggests that that experience is a dubious legacy handed down through generations of mothers and daughters. Teaching "That soft Answers turn away Wrath" is a lesson central to the traditional education of daughters by mothers. As in Laetitia's childhood story, only "soft answers" can turn male aggressors into protectors; what they protect women from, of course, is other male aggressors.

"The autobiographer's 'fiction,' " writes Patricia Meyer Spacks, "is stronger and more telling than his 'truth.' "[42] No doubt she intends the pun on "telling," a pun which implies that telling is the purpose of autobiography: the writer needs to tell and the reader needs to be told. What does Mrs. Pilkington's autobiography tell us that could not have been told by a "factual" account of the events of her life? No factual rendering of events could have satisfactorily conveyed to us her struggle to assert her identity in a society that threatened to erase women who did not conform to at least one of the roles prefabricated for them; probably the most important reason for this is that no language for this phenomenon existed during the eighteenth century. In order to identify this fear of erasure, we need to know that Laetitia was obsessed with doubles to the point where she even invented them. These doubles are like mirror images: they may be illusory but they nevertheless confirm her existence in the world. What we also need to know that no factual account of her life can give us is the intensely claustrophobic nature of the dilemma she was in. The range of options she had was as narrow as the options themselves. Forced by circumstance out of the role of daughter/wife/mother, she had the option of either occupying the role of "profligate whore," as Swift labeled her, or carving out an identity for herself in that no-woman's land—the land of invisible women—that lay between the recognized categories of "virtue" and "infamy." The inclusion, invention, and even outright borrowing of incidents of entrapment and enclosure demonstrate how intensely she experienced the narrowness of her options.

The impossibility of coming to any sound conclusion about the "real" Mrs. Pilkington has little to do with where the line between autobiography and fiction lies in the *Memoirs,* and much to do with the fact that Laetitia herself never found a way out of her identity dilemma. Spacks says it well when she writes of Laetitia Pilkington that "However indistinct her version of her being, she can yet interpret herself as heroine, forced by events to behave sometimes in dubious ways, but pure in heart and womanly in intent if not in action. Her prose converts her into a person of significance, defending her against the world's reluctance to take her seriously."[43] But by taking her seriously now—as a woman and as a writer—we can at least come to a better understanding of her and of a whole generation of literary women.

NOTES

INTRODUCTION

1. "The Introduction," in *The Poems of Anne Countess of Winchilsea,* ed. Myra Reynolds (1903; rpt. New York: AMS Press, 1974), p. 4.

2. Quoted in Miss [Anne Isabella] Thackeray, *A Book of Sibyls* (London: Smith Elder, 1883), p. 41.

3. I mention here only basic positions and representative critics. For summaries and analyses of these and other views on the issue, see Toril Moi, *Sexual/Textual Politics: Feminist Literary Theory* (London and New York: Methuen, 1985).

4. Mary Ellmann, *Thinking about Women* (New York: Harcourt, Brace, and World, 1968), pp. 156–58; Ellmann cites very little evidence for this intriguing idea, however.

CHAPTER I

1. *Monthly Review* (June 1764), 445–50.

2. See my forthcoming biography of Mary Whateley Darwall.

3. Mary Scott, *The Female Advocate; A Poem, Occasioned by Reading Mr. Duncombe's Feminead,* intro. Gae Holladay (Los Angeles: William Andrews Clark Memorial Library, 1984), pp. 26–27.

4. See, for example, C. V. Deane, *Aspects of Eighteenth-Century Nature Poetry* (1935; rpt. New York: Barnes and Noble, 1968), p. 138; C. E. de Haas, *Nature and the Country in English Poetry of the First Half of the Eighteenth Century* (Amsterdam: H. J. Paris, 1928), p. 192.

5. Biographical information is from Marjorie Williams, *William Shenstone: A Chapter in Eighteenth-Century Taste* (Birmingham: Cornish Brothers, 1935).

6. Unpublished letter from Shenstone to Mrs. Bennett, dated 30 October 1761, in the archives of the Birmingham Reference Library.

7. [Mary Whateley], *Original Poems on Several Occasions* (London: R. and J. Dodsley, 1764), "Elegy Written in a Garden," p. 56; "To the Rev. Mr. Welchman at Tanworth," p. 90; "The Vanity of external Accomplishments," p. 102. All references are to this edition and appear in the text.

8. Shenstone wrote a poem on his own indolence; his letters bear out that characterization. Miss Whateley's handwriting is energetic, even aggressive; her six children and the activities mentioned in her later book of poems (1794) bear witness to her energy as well.

9. *The Works in Verse and Prose of William Shenstone, Esq.*, 2 vols. (London: R. and J. Dodsley, 1764), 1:6; Dodsley's note (1:4) dates the essay twenty years before publication of the book. All references are to this edition and appear in the text.

10. He does sometimes mention the Muse, as in Elegy 3 where she is "virtue's friend" and possesses persuasive powers; there, however, he is speaking of a dead fellow poet. Typically, he credits *poetry* with active power.

11. Four stanzas set the scene; six describe improper subjects; three address the clergyman. Only four out of seventeen describe both the purpose and proper topics of poetry.

12. Whateley, "To the Rev. Mr. Welchman at Tanworth," pp. 90–94.

13. *The Letters of William Shenstone*, ed. Duncan Mallam (Minneapolis: University of Minnesota Press, 1939), pp. 401–2.

14. Generally speaking, the personal, confessional mode of Miss Whateley's poetry is unmistakable. She did decorously explain that her love poems were all "Fictions" (p. 6), but perhaps they too are "sincere," though too few facts about her life have survived to support autobiographical reading of all the poems. Shenstone claimed that "particular incidents in life" suggested the subjects of his poems (1:10), and modern critics agree in reading his poems autobiographically.

15. See, for example, Geoffrey Tillotson, "William Shenstone," in *Essays in Criticism and Research* (Cambridge: Cambridge University Press; New York: Macmillan, 1942), pp. 105–10.

16. I argue this point in my forthcoming biography of Mary Whateley Darwall.

17. *Poems (1686) by Mrs. Anne Killigrew*, intro. Richard Morton (Gainesville, Fla.: Scholars' Facsimiles and Reprints, 1967), p. 58.

18. I follow here the order in which the poems appear in the book. It is not possible to establish the chronology of composition.

19. C. A. Moore, "Whig Panegyric Verse, 1700–1760: A Phase of Sentimentalism," *PMLA*, 41 (1926), 362–401; for Shenstone, see especially p. 395.

20. *The Poetical Works of William Shenstone*, ed. George Gilfillan (Edinburgh: Nichol, 1854), p. xix.

21. A. R. Humphreys, *William Shenstone: An Eighteenth-Century Portrait* (Cambridge: Cambridge University Press, 1937), p. 69.

22. Whateley, "Elegy on leaving ———," pp. 34–35.

23. *Critical Review* (August 1764), 115.

24. For further argument that this poem is an allegory, see my "Women Poets and the Pastoral Trap: The Case of Mary Whateley," in *Eighteenth-Century Women and the Arts*, ed. Frederick M. Keener and Susan E. Lorsch (New York, Westport, London: Greenwood Press, 1988), pp. 93–105.

25. Sylvia H. Myers, "Learning, Virtue, and the Term 'Bluestocking,' " in *Studies in Eighteenth-Century Culture*, vol. 15, ed. O. M. Brack, Jr. (Madison: University of Wisconsin Press, 1986), pp. 279–88, especially p. 281.

26. Myra Reynolds, Lady Winchilsea's editor, implies that all her poems were "written after 1685," that is, after her marriage—but gives no evidence to support this (*The Poems of Anne Countess of Winchilsea* [1903; rpt. New York: AMS Press, 1974], p. xvii); Lady Winchilsea herself, in her prose "Preface," says that prudence did not "lett any attempts of mine in Poetry, shew themselves whilst I liv'd . . . in Court." (p. 7). See also my "Publishing without Perishing: Lady Winchilsea's *Miscellany Poems* of 1713," *Restoration*, 5, No. 1 (Spring 1981), 27–37.

CHAPTER 2

1. *The Poems of Anne, Countess of Winchilsea*, ed. Myra Reynolds (1903; rpt. New York: AMS Press, 1974). In her introduction, pp. li–lxxxiii, Reynolds gives a history of the commentary

on the poems from Anne Finch's own age to Saintsbury in 1898. Further references to Anne Finch's poems are to this edition and appear in the text.

2. Frank Kermode, *The Genesis of Secrecy: On the Interpretation of Narrative* (Cambridge: Harvard University Press, 1979), p. 5.

3. For a study of Anne Finch and the conventions that is not concerned with her gender, see Reuben A. Brower, "Lady Winchilsea and the Poetic Tradition of the Seventeenth Century," *Studies in Philology,* 42 (1945), 61–80.

4. Paul Fussell, *Samuel Johnson and the Life of Writing* (London: Chatto and Windus, 1972), p. 37.

5. Anne Bradstreet, *Poems,* ed. Robert Hutchinson (New York: Dover, 1969), p. 118. Further references to Anne Bradstreet's poems are to this edition and appear in the text.

6. In this instance and hereafter I use the words "diminish" and "diminishing" as terms in rhetoric applied to epithets and figures intended, within the decorum of the poem, to debase, lower, or demean. Thus, in a conventional "praise," the poet would choose words to augment or elevate her subject; in a conventional "contempt," the poet would select diminishing words.

7. *The World Split Open: Four Centuries of Women Poets in England and America,* ed. Louise Bernikow (New York: Vintage/Random, 1974), p. 80. Further references to Anne Killigrew's poems are to this edition and appear in the text.

8. This idea is derived from the concept of "inversion" in Annette Kolodny, "Some Notes on Defining a Feminist Literary Criticism," *Critical Inquiry,* 2, No. 1 (1975), 80–81.

9. Earl Miner, *The Restoration Mode from Milton to Dryden* (Princeton: Princeton University Press, 1974), pp. 3–50.

10. Kermode, p. 18.

11. For the purposes of this essay, I have taken the whole canon of Anne Finch's work as a unit, disregarding the differences between her published and unpublished poems. For a study of those differences, see Ann Messenger, "Publishing Without Perishing: Lady Winchilsea's *Miscellany Poems* of 1713," *Restoration,* 5, No. 1 (Spring 1981), 27–37.

12. My analysis of Anne Finch's relation to the traditions of English love poetry accords with the views expressed by Katharine Rogers in her essay "Anne Finch, Countess of Winchilsea: An Augustan Woman Poet," in *Shakespeare's Sisters: Feminist Essays on Women Poets,* ed. Sandra Gilbert and Susan Gubar (Bloomington: Indiana University Press, 1979), pp. 32–46. Her comments on the strong moral position informing "Ardelia's Answer to Ephelia," her judgment that "A Noctural Reverie" is written in the Augustan mode, her observations on the differences in Anne Finch's handling of the conventions of the poem of retirement, and her interpretation of "The Bird and the Arras" as an emblem of the poet's sense of herself, all concur with my comments on these poems, though she goes rather farther than I do in her reading of the last-mentioned poem as an allegory. For the sake of brevity, I list our agreements here. The fact that two critics have independently reached similar understandings of the same texts strengthens our shared positions.

13. Ann Messenger, " 'Adam Pos'd': Metaphysical and Augustan Satire," *West Coast Review,* 8, No. 4 (1974), 10.

14. Ruth Wallerstein, " 'On the Death of Mrs. Killigrew': The Perfecting of a Genre," in *Seventeenth-Century English Poetry: Modern Essays in Criticism,* ed. William R. Keast, rev. ed. (New York: Oxford University Press, 1962), p. 458.

15. Maren-Sofie Røstvig, *The Happy Man,* Vol. 1 (Trondheim, Norway: Norwegian University Press, 1962), p. 318.

16. Ibid.

17. Northrop Frye, *The Well-Tempered Critic* (Bloomington: Indiana University Press, 1963), pp. 99–100.

18. Donald Davie, *Purity of Diction in English Verse* (New York: Oxford, 1953), p. 55.

19. Røstvig, pp. 7–52 *passim*.

20. Ellen Moers, *Literary Women: The Great Writers* (New York: Doubleday, 1976), pp. 245–51. In these pages in the section of her book called "Metaphors: A Postlude," Moers speculates about the bird, especially the caged or imprisoned bird, as a metaphor in women's writing.

21. Ann Messenger, "Selected Nightingales and an 'Augustan' Sensibility," *English Studies in Canada*, 6 (1980), 145–53.

22. For a recent commentary on the poem, somewhat different from mine, see Lucy Brashear, "Finch's 'The Bird and the Arras,' " *Explicator*, 39, No. 3 (1981), 21–22.

23. John Goode, "Women and the Literary Text," in *The Rights and Wrongs of Women*, ed. J. Mitchell and A. Oakley (Harmondsworth, England: Penguin, 1976), p. 218.

CHAPTER 3

My research on Mary Pix was supported in part by a Bert Henry Memorial Scholarship from Simon Fraser University and was carried out at the Henry E. Huntington Library, San Marino, California, with the assistance of their incomparable facilities and helpful staff. I am most grateful to both institutions.

1. For a detailed discussion of the split between the theaters and the history of the Lincoln's Inn Fields players, see Judith Milhous, *Thomas Betterton and the Management of Lincoln's Inn Fields, 1695–1708* (Carbondale: Southern Illinois University Press, 1979).

2. *The Female Wits* (1704; rpt. intro. Lucyle Hook, Augustan Reprint Series, no. 120, Los Angeles: William Andrews Clark Memorial Library, University of California at Los Angeles, 1967). Constance Clark in her recent work, *Three Augustan Women Playwrights* (New York: Peter Lang, 1986), rejects the traditional production date of this play, arguing that the textual reference to *The World in the Moon* would date it to mid-1697 (see Clark, pp. 289–90). I am not fully convinced, as she ignores some information about the production in presenting her ideas.

3. For a more complete discussion of marriage law and custom in this period, see Lawrence Stone, *The Family, Sex and Marriage in England, 1500–1800* (New York: Harper and Row, 1977), especially chapter 7; Gellert S. Alleman, *Matrimonial Law and the Materials of Restoration Comedy* (Wallingford, Pa.: n.p., 1942); and Peter Malekin, *Liberty and Love: English Literature and Society, 1640–88* (New York: St. Martins, 1981).

4. Susan Staves, *Players' Sceptres: Fictions of Authority in the Restoration* (Lincoln: University of Nebraska Press, 1979), pp. 111–13; see also Stone, pp. 265–66.

5. For example, F. W. Bateson, *English Comic Drama, 1700–1750* (1929; rpt. New York: Russell and Russell, 1963), pp. 61–77. John Palmer, *The Comedy of Manners* (1913; rpt. New York: Russell and Russell, 1962), is more typical of post-Victorians who mention no women writers at all. Kenneth Muir devotes two sentences to Aphra Behn (no one else appears) in his *The Comedy of Manners* (London: Hutchinson, 1970), p. 66. *From Dryden to Johnson*, ed. Boris Ford, vol. 4 of *The Pelican Guide to English Literature* (Harmondsworth, England: Penguin, 1951), includes a survey by A. R. Humphreys, "The Literary Scene," in which he takes care of the women writers in one sentence: "To venture into the comedy of Cibber, Mrs. Centlivre and Steele is to descend too far into the second-rate" (p. 92); then he goes on to find value in the work of Cibber and Steele. In the bibliographic appendix to this work by C. J. Horne, Aphra Behn is described as having an "obscure and probably improper early career" (p. 466). Allardyce Nicoll (*A History of Early Eighteenth Century Drama, 1700–1750*, 2nd ed. [Cambridge: Cambridge University Press, 1929]) is a good deal more balanced in his views and more enthusiastic about Mrs. Centlivre than the critics named above, but even he accepts a suggestion that she had help from a man with her *A Bold Stroke for a Wife* (p. 156). Robert Hume (*The Development of English Drama in the Late Seventeenth Century* [Ox-

ford: Clarendon, 1976]), is a careful scholar offering many detailed and reasonable criticisms of the period, but with an evident preference for earlier "hard" comedies such as those of Aphra Behn. He is severe with the women he describes as attempting "new" comedy (pp. 421–22).

6. Feminism as an idea and a label is both general and complex in its possible meanings. Definitions of the term seem often to depend upon a particular historical context or the personal bias of the writer and have filled whole volumes of discussion and argument. Without attempting any closure of discussion and for the purposes of this essay, I venture to suggest that one reasonable definition of "feminism" is that attitude women in any age or society may have which determines them to place their own self-respect and self-development ahead of their duties and obligations toward men; which causes them to support and cherish other women in the face of social oppression and male domination; and which makes them advocates of social changes that will improve women's lives. By this definition feminism is neither a nineteenth- nor a twentieth-century invention, but a much older phenomenon which may be observed in many times and cultures.

7. Nancy Cotton, *Women Playwrights* (Lewisburg, Pa.: Bucknell University Press, 1980), pp. 180–212.

8. Cotton, pp. 181–82, citing *A Journal from Parnassus* (1688; rpt. London: P. J. Dobell, 1937), pp. 25–27.

9. Gerard Langbaine [and Charles Gildon], *Lives and Characters of the English Dramatick Poets* (London: n.p., 1699); Giles Jacob, *The Poetical Register: On the Lives and Characters of the English Dramatic Poets*, 2nd ed. (1719; rpt. London: n.p., 1720).

10. John Genest, ed., *Some Account of the English Stage from the Restoration in 1660 to 1830*, 10 vols. (1832; rpt. New York: Burt Franklin, 1967); Dr. [John] Doran, *"Their Majesties' Servants": Annals of the English Stage, from Thomas Betterton to Edmund Kean*, 3 vols. (1847; rpt. New York: Widdleton, 1865).

11. Margaret L. McDonald, *The Independent Woman*, Salzburg Studies in English, no. 32 (Salzburg: Institut für englische Sprache und Literatur, 1976).

12. Fidelis Morgan, *The Female Wits* (London: Virago, 1981).

13. Staves, particularly pp. 169–89.

14. Jean Gagen, *The New Woman* (New York: Twayne, 1954), pp. 58–61.

15. Gagen, pp. 82–83.

16. Edna L. Steeves, *The Plays of Mary Pix and Catharine Trotter*, 2 vols. (New York: Garland, 1982), pp. xi–lxi.

17. One play sometimes attributed to Pix, which she does not include in her edition, is *Zelmane; or, The Corinthian Queen* (1704). Constance Clark argues for the attribution in her work on Pix.

18. Paula Louise Barbour, "A Critical Edition of Mary Pix's *The Spanish Wives*" (Ph.D. dissertation, Yale University, 1975); and "Mary Pix, 1666–1709?—The Losing of a Playwright" (Paper presented at the annual meeting of the American Society for Eighteenth-Century Studies, Chicago, 1978).

19. Constance Clark, *Three Augustan Women Playwrights* (New York: Peter Lang, 1986).

20. Hume, p. 419.

21. Eliza Haywood, *A Wife to be Lett* (London: Brown and Chapman, 1724).

22. For all theaters, dates, and other production information in this essay, see *The London Stage 1660–1800, Part 1: 1660–1700*, ed. William Van Lennep (Carbondale: Southern Illinois University Press, 1965) and *Part 2: 1700–1729*, ed. Emmett L. Avery, vol. 1 (Carbondale: Southern Illinois University Press, 1960), hereinafter cited as *LS, 1* and *LS, 2*.

23. Staves, pp. 160–61.

24. For a discussion of this custom see John Loftis, *Politics of Drama in Augustan England* (Oxford: Clarendon, 1963), pp. 7–34.

25. For a detailed discussion of the influence of Spanish plays and Spanish ideas of honor in the English theater, see John Loftis, *The Spanish Plays of Neoclassical England* (New Haven: Yale University Press, 1973). A contemporary record of the prevalence of these ideas may be found in "The Brawny Bishop's Complaint" (1699; rpt. in *Poems on Affairs of State: Augustan Satirical Verse, 1660–1714, VI: 1697–1704,* ed. Frank H. Ellis [New Haven: Yale University Press, 1970], p. 42).

26. All quotations from plays by Mary Pix are taken from the Garland edition (1982), edited by Steeves. Specific references to these plays are cited in the body of the paper by act and page number, as divisions into scenes are erratic in the original texts. Pagination of the reprint edition is based on the first editions of individual plays. Spelling and punctuation have been regularized where necessary for clarity.

27. Colley Cibber, in his *Apology for the Life of Mr. Colley Cibber, Written by Himself* (1740; rpt. ed. R. W. Lowe, 2nd. ed., 2 vols., London: J. M. Dent, 1914), I: 102–6, describes the struggles of the few and unskilled actors at Drury Lane in the early years of the split between the companies; see also *A Comparison between the Two Stages,* ed. Staring B. Wells (1942; rpt. New York: Benjamin Blom, 1971), p. 7. The quotation is from Jacob, p. 203.

28. Genest, 2:32–83, supplements the production information given in *LS, 1. The Spanish Wives* was also performed in Dublin in 1707–8; see Wm. Smith Clark, *The Early Irish Stage* (Oxford: Clarendon, 1955), p. 124.

29. John Loftis, *Comedy and Society* (Stanford: Stanford University Press, 1959), p. 43.

30. Although such social changes, not yet reflected in law, can be extremely difficult to document, Stone's study seems to argue for a pattern of change in this area. See particularly his chapter on "Companionate Marriage," especially pp. 340–41, and his references to the Filmer-Locke debate (pp. 265–66). Daniel Defoe's argument for companionate marriage, discussed by David Blewett in "Changing Attitudes toward Marriage in the Time of Defoe: The Case of *Moll Flanders*," *Huntington Library Quarterly,* 44 (1981), 77–88, also supports the notion that greater equality between husbands and wives and marriage contracted for affection was much more likely in the decades after 1688. Malekin remarks on the post-Restoration retreat from the Civil War and Interregnum trend toward greater freedom for women (pp. 188–94), but does not refer to the articulate feminism of the 1680s and 1690s nor does he go on to discuss general changes in society for women after 1688.

31. See Loftis, *Comedy and Society,* p. 25, and Joseph Wood Krutch, *Comedy and Conscience after the Restoration* (1924; rpt. New York: Russell and Russell, 1967), pp. 94–101, for discussions of attacks on the theater before Jeremy Collier.

32. Dudley Bahlman, *The Moral Revolution of 1688* (New Haven: Yale University Press, 1957), pp. 18–19, 31–37.

33. For references to this changing audience see: Harold Love, "Who Were the Restoration Audience?" *Yearbook of English Studies,* 10 (1980), 21–44, especially p. 29, which also refers to essays by John Loftis and John Harrington Smith on this topic; and Arthur H. Scouten and Robert D. Hume, " 'Restoration Comedy' and Its Audiences, 1660–1776," *Yearbook of English Studies,* 10 (1980), 45–69.

34. Henry William Pedicord, "The Changing Audience," in *The London Theatre World, 1660–1800,* ed. Robert D. Hume (Carbondale: Southern Illinois University Press, 1980), p. 240.

35. Scouten and Hume, p. 59. They also refer here to the "failure of . . . new plays [which] reflects the authors' inability to find any formula which would please the audience."

36. John Vanbrugh would be an exception to this norm. The character study of his heroine in *The Provoked Wife* is so unusual in this regard that it is hardly possible to classify the play as a comedy in the traditional sense. In fact it seems clear that Vanbrugh was the inventor of the psychological drama, a genre not even recognized until much later.

37. Staves, pp. 179–80; Hume, pp. 386–87.

38. Quotations from the play are from *The Wives' Excuse* (London: W. Freeman, 1692).

39. Hume, p. 382; for his discussion of Vanbrugh see pp. 413–15.

40. Staves, pp. 177–79, 176.

41. Examples of contemporary misogynist satire are discussed at length in Felicity Nussbaum's study of late seventeenth- and early eighteenth-century satires against women, *The Brink of All We Hate* (Lexington: University Press of Kentucky, 1984). See also *Court Satires of the Restoration*, ed. John Harold Wilson (Columbus: Ohio State University Press, 1976) for examples of satiric attacks on actresses.

42. Robert Gould, *Poems*, 2nd ed. (London: n.p., 1689), pp. 161–85, 55.

43. Examples of these occur in such comedies as Thomas Wright's *The Virtuoso's* (a 1693 adaptation of Molière) and D'Urfey's *The Richmond Heiress* (1693), in which the modest heroine makes no pretense to wit, while clever but immoral women fail to attract the lovers of their choice. For a more complete discussion of this point see Gagen, pp. 55–65.

44. For detailed description of the failure of new work at this time see Milhous, pp. 102–3.

45. Both plays, in a time when many beginners simply did adaptations or translations of other works, are evidently her own, although Nancy Cotton describes *Ibrahim* as modeled on a play by Fletcher (Cotton, p. 89); Giles Jacob alludes only to novels as sources of her plots (Jacob, pp. 203–4).

46. The author of that piece, incidentally, was a friend of the Drury Lane circle of wits and actors; his only play for the Patent Company had been a failure (see *LS, 1*, p. 453).

47. Jacob, p. 204.

48. Satires on Elizabeth Barry and biographical notes are to be found in Wilson, *Court Satires:* "On Three Late Marriages" (1682), pp. 76–80 and notes to p. 76; "The Session of Ladies" (April 1688), pp. 204–16; and "Satire on Benting" (March 1689), pp. 217–25 and notes to pp. 224–25; see also Gould's "Playhouse," in *Poems*, pp. 180–85. See Milhous, p. 99, for Barry's reaction to some of this.

49. For various aspects of and reactions to the charge of plagiarism against Powell and the row which resulted, see *LS, 1;* Cotton, pp. 112, 114; the dedication by Mary Pix to her own play, *The Deceiver Deceived* (1698); the anonymous *Animadversions on Mr. Congreve's Late Answer to Mr. Collier* (1698; rpt. New York: Garland, 1972), p. 34. The continuation of Langbaine's *Lives and Characters of the English Dramatick Poets*, usually attributed to Charles Gildon, lists the disputed work as belonging to Mary Pix and does not include Powell's version among his attributed plays, even though Gildon and Powell were associates in the Drury Lane Theatre Company.

50. Elizabeth Barry's power to sponsor plays in the Lincoln's Inn Fields Company is described by Milhous, pp. 83, 98–99, 101, 161.

51. The discovery of Dancourt as Pix's source should, I believe, be credited to Cotton, p. 116, as it was evidently not known before: see Nicoll, p. 171. Florent Carton Dancourt, *Le Chevalier à la Mode*, in *Chefs-D'Oeuvre des Auteurs Comiques* (Paris: Fermin Didot Frères, 1860), 2: 3–92. Translation within this essay is my own.

52. Cotton, p. 116.

53. Bahlman, pp. 93–97.

54. Milhous, pp. 119–50.

55. *A Comparison*, ed. Staring B. Wells, p. 14. I have modernized spelling and punctuation.

56. Milhous, p. 152.

57. Among these women were such writers as Sarah Fyge Field Egerton, Jane Barker, Mary Astell, Judith Drake, and Lady Mary Chudleigh. Examples of these efforts have been pub-

lished in *First Feminists: British Women Writers, 1578–1799,* ed. Moira Ferguson (Bloomington: Indiana University Press, 1985), pp. 152–238.

58. Thomas Wright, *Country Conversations* (London: n.p., 1693).

59. Colly Cibber, *The Careless Husband,* ed. William Appleton (Lincoln: University of Nebraska Press, 1966).

60. Milhous, p. 188.

61. *National Union Catalogue: Pre-1956 Imprints,* vol. 460 (n.p.: Mansell, 1976).

62. "The Tryal of Skill, or A New Session of the Poets, Calculated for the Meridian of Parnassus" (1704), rpt. in *Poems on Affairs of State,* vol. 7, pp. 679–711, incl. notes.

63. The verses for Higgons are mentioned in *A Comparison,* p. 45.

64. Genest, 2: 354.

65. Cibber, *Apology,* 1: 321–22.

66. Milhous, pp. 199, 200.

67. John Downes, *Roscius Anglicanus* (1708; rpt. with James Wright, *Historia Histrionica,* New York: Garland, 1974), p. 48.

68. Genest, 2: 331–32.

69. *The Daily Courant* (19 July 1705), quoted by Milhous, p. 200.

70. Downes, p. 50, mentions the first temporary reunion of October, 1706; this whole period is detailed in Milhous, pp. 201–10.

71. Milhous, p. 205; Genest, 2: 353.

72. For a discussion of the split in performance between Drury Lane and Lincoln's Inn Fields, see Staring B. Wells's notes to his edition of *A Comparison,* p. 123.

73. Genest, 2: 291.

74. For comparisons of their stage life, see *LS, 2.*

75. Milhous talks about the more limited number of people employed by the united companies after the reunion, pp. 213–14.

76. *Animadversions,* p. 34.

77. *A Comparison,* ed. Staring B. Wells, p. 46.

78. *The Town Display'd, in a Letter to Amintor in the Country* (London: n.p., 1701), p. 16.

79. Dramatis personae to *The Female Wits,* in Morgan, p. 392.

80. *LS, 2,* p. 193. The announcement quoted from the *Post Boy,* 26–28 May 1709, has never been taken seriously so far as I have been able to discover: " 'the greatest part of which said Comedy [*The Busie Body*], and also that of the *Gamester,* was wrote by the said Mrs. Pix.' " A more likely supposition is that the help she was probably given as a newcomer to the company between 1700 and 1706 was the source of Centlivre's natural feeling of indebtedness. Clark discusses the probable friendship between Pix and Centlivre in some detail (pp. 200–2).

CHAPTER 4

1. Donald A. Stauffer, *The Art of Biography in Eighteenth Century England* (Princeton: Princeton University Press, 1941), p. 69. Madame d'Aulnoy's memoirs appeared originally as *Mémoires de la Comtesse d'Aulnoy* (Paris: C. Barbin, 1690); the second edition, in English, appeared as Part 1 of *The Diverting Works of the Countess d'Anois, Author of the Ladies Travels to Spain* (London: J. Nicholson, 1707).

2. Ibid., p. 66.

3. Ibid., p. 3.

4. *The Parallel; or Pilkington and Phillips Compared* (London: M. Cooper, 1748), written by "an Oxford Scholar," is a relatively tasteful and reasoned literary appreciation of both memoirs.

The author points out that Mrs. Pilkington has a tendency to exaggerate, that she is often indelicate in her disclosures, and that her poetry is less skilled than her prose. He thinks she is a very evocative writer and that she is often exactly right in her presentation of character. He does not consider the *Memoirs* scandalous or harmful but accepts that memoirists are "compelled by an invincible Necessity to make their Writings of some Use" as instruction (p. 23). This pamphlet was so mild in comparison to all the other criticism that poured out from the presses, that Mrs. Pilkington hardly knew how to respond to it at first. However, she soon recovered from her bewilderment and attacked the pamphlet viciously for ten pages (*Memoirs*, 2: 349–59).

5. *The Memoirs of Mrs. Laetitia Pilkington, Written by Herself*, 3 vols. (1748–54; rpt. New York: Garland Publishing, 1975), 1: 2. All further references are to this edition and appear in the text. All biographical facts, unless otherwise noted, are from the *Memoirs*.

6. In *The Curious Art of Autobiography* (New York: Philosophical Library, 1956), N. H. Wethered writes: "By an odd coincidence [Edward] Gibbon's *Autobiography* and Boswell's *Life of Johnson* appeared within two years of each other. The coincidence is all the more striking since the two works are probably the best examples of autobiography and biography in the language" (pp. 56–57). The characteristics of these two works set the standards for subsequent life-writings. Both are of the "life-and-times" variety with much emphasis on the "times." (Or, to be more precise, Boswell's *Life* is a "life-and-circle" biography which has been useful to generations of eighteenth-century scholars as a kind of "Who's Who" of the Johnson era.) Perhaps this is why even Colley Cibber's *Apology*, in spite of Cibber's vanity and his highly idiosyncratic style, has gone through sixteen editions since its appearance in 1740; it is invaluable as a history of the theater during Cibber's long lifetime. Jean Jacques Rousseau's *Confessions*, although highly introspective, are set against the background of one of the most exciting periods in French history. As makers and/or chroniclers of history, these highly successful men played significant roles in the eighteenth century, and therefore their autobiographies are valued. Gibbon, Cibber, and Rousseau were all meticulous in their attention to detail, careful in the construction of their narratives around one central theme (i.e., their professions), and relatively reticent about the intimate details of their domestic lives. These and other criteria of form and content are the subject of Wayne Shumaker's *English Autobiography: Its Emergence, Materials, and Form* (Berkeley and Los Angeles: University of California Press, 1954). Shumaker is taken to task by Estelle Jelinek in her "Introduction: Women's Autobiography and the Male Tradition" (*Women's Autobiography*, ed. Estelle C. Jelinek [Bloomington: Indiana University Press, 1980]); she contends that "Despite the fact that women's life studies are excluded from the evidence from which the characteristics of the genre are drawn, it is assumed that they will either conform to them or else be disqualified as autobiographies" (p. 6).

7. Stauffer, p. 386.

8. Samuel Johnson, *Idler* essay for 24 November 1759; rpt. in *The Idler*, 2 vols. (London: F. Power and Co., 1790), 2: 147–48.

9. Arthur Melville Clark, *Autobiography: Its Genesis and Phases* (Edinburgh: Oliver and Boyd, 1935), p. 20.

10. Roy Pascal, *Design and Truth in Autobiography* (Cambridge: Harvard University Press, 1960), p. 63.

11. Ibid., p. 83.

12. *Thraliana: The Diary of Mrs. Hester Lynch Thrale, 1776–1809*, ed. Katherine Balderston, 2 vols. (1946; rpt. Oxford: Clarendon, 1951), 1: 426.

13. *Dictionary of National Biography*, 22 vols. (London: Oxford University Press, 1917), 15: 1182.

14. Elizabeth Montagu, quoted in "Bibliographical Note," *The Memoirs of Mrs. Laetitia Pilkington, Written by Herself*, ed. Iris Barry (London: George Routledge and Sons, 1928), pp. 471–72.

15. Virginia Woolf, "The Lives of the Obscure," in *The Common Reader*, 1st series (1925; rpt. London: Hogarth Press, 1962), pp. 146–67. Iris Barry, introduction to *The Memoirs of Mrs. Laetitia Pilkington* (1928), pp. 1–24. Walter and Clare Jerrold, "Letitia Pilkington: Swift's 'Insolent Slut,' " in *Five Queer Women* (London: Brentano's, 1929), pp. 276–346. Lord Ponsonby, "Laetitia Pilkington (1712–1750)—a Curiosity of Literature," *English*, 1, No. 4 (1937), 297–306.

16. Barry, p. 10.

17. Ponsonby, p. 298.

18. Ibid., p. 297.

19. Jerrold, p. 276.

20. Barry, p. 24.

21. Ibid., p. 17.

22. Woolf, p. 161.

23. Jelinek, pp. 7–8.

24. Patricia Meyer Spacks, *Imagining a Self: Autobiography and Novel in Eighteenth-Century England* (Cambridge: Harvard University Press, 1976), p. 15.

25. Ibid., p. 88.

26. Cynthia Pomerleau, "The Emergence of Women's Autobiography in England," in *Women's Autobiography*, ed. Jelinek, p. 37.

27. Woolf, p. 161.

28. Jerrold, p. 299.

29. Barry, p. 8.

30. Lord Bolingbroke, quoted in Ibid., p. 8.

31. This account of Matthew Pilkington's activities in London on Swift's behalf relies heavily on Barry, pp. 1–7.

32. Spacks, p. 81.

33. *The Correspondence of Jonathan Swift*, ed. F. Elrington Ball, 6 vols. (London: G. Bell and Sons, 1910–14), 6: 68–69.

34. *Notes and Queries* (27 July 1912), 66. In his memoirs, the second son, John Carteret Pilkington, corroborates in general terms his mother's opinion of Matthew Pilkington's character. Although John clearly takes Laetitia's part, he does insist that Matthew became a negligent and cruel father only after he met the unpleasant woman who was to become his second wife. John recalls that his parents' separation occurred when he was six or seven years old, and reluctantly gives his father the benefit of the doubt regarding Laetitia's alleged adultery. Matthew's mistress did not care for his children, and consequently they were eventually fostered by various Van Lewen and Pilkington relatives. Matthew disowned John when, in his early teens, he left Matthew's house to live with one of Laetitia's uncles (*The Real Story of John Carteret Pilkington, written by Himself* [London, 1760]). John eventually joined his mother in London, accompanied her back to Ireland, and after her death wrote an appendix to the manuscript for Laetitia's third volume.

35. Lee R. Edwards, in "Flights of Angels: Varieties of a Fictional Paradigm" (*Feminist Studies*, 5, No. 3 [Fall 1979], 548–70), discusses the limitations imposed upon women writers by traditional literary forms, and examines the ways in which women subvert forms to reflect female experience more accurately. Perhaps the fullest exploration of this literary phenomenon as well as women's use of doubles and the recurring images of entrapment and enclosure is Sandra Gilbert and Susan Gubar's *The Madwoman in the Attic: The Woman Writer and the Nineteenth-Century Literary Imagination* (New Haven: Yale University Press, 1979). The chapter on Jane Austen entitled "Shut Up in Prose" is particularly useful in relating these themes to the eighteenth-century woman writer.

36. This interpretation of the double as both Self and Other was first suggested to me by an article which predates Gilbert and Gubar's *Madwoman*. In "The Double in Twentieth Century Women's Poetry" (*Atlantis*, 2, No. 2 [Spring 1977], 95–110), Jean Mallinson writes that "the

Double in literature stands for unlived life, for the unmanifest side of one's nature: the latent or unexpressed embodied as Other" (p. 95).

37. The establishment which Mrs. Pilkington calls "White's Chocolate House" was actually White's Club, the first gentleman's club in London.

38. *The Correspondence of Samuel Richardson*, ed. Anna Laetitia Barbauld, 6 vols. (1804; rpt. New York: AMS Press, 1966), 2: 137.

39. Ibid., pp. 138–39.

40. For example, Richardson's Mrs. Jewkes (*Pamela*).

41. "The Apotheosis of Milton," *The Gentleman's Magazine* (September 1738), 469. I am indebted to Ann Messenger for bringing this article to my attention.

42. Spacks, p. 18.

43. Ibid., p. 16.

INDEX

The manuscript was edited by Robin DuBlanc.
The book was designed by Selma Tenenbaum.
The typeface for the text is Garamond.
The display face is DeVinne Ornamental
and Garamond Ultra Condensed.
Manufactured in the United States of America.